Character Education Workbook

for
School Boards,
Administrators &
Community Leaders

Judith B. Hoffman & Anne R. Lee

Series Editor — Dr. Philip Fitch Vincent
Text Editing — Dr. Ruth C. Walden
Text design — Kati Severa
Cover design — Paul Turley

Quantity Purchases
Schools, schoolboards, professional groups, clubs and other organizations may qualify for special terms when ordering quantities of this or other CDG titles. For ordering information contact the Sales Department, Character Development Group, P.O. Box 9211, Chapel Hill, NC 27515-9211

(919) 967-2110, or fax us at (919) 967-2139

ISBN: 0-9653163-2-7 $12.00

Character Development Group is an educator resource organization that offers publications and staff development training for the planning, implementation and assessment of effective, results-producing character education programs in schools and school systems. For more information, call us at (919) 967-2110, or e-mail us at respect96@aol.com.

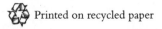 Printed on recycled paper

"*Nothing* is more important for the public weal than to form and train up youth in **wisdom** and **virtue**."

Benjamin Franklin

DEDICATION

To our families:

Judy: husband Paul and children Jennifer
and husband Paul, Sarah
and husband Lee, Rachel, Joseph
and grandson Garrett

Anne: husband Whit and children
Justin, Elizabeth, Jonathan and Kathryn

To all children around the world who
need the commitment of adults
in their lives to demonstrate and teach
good character

ACKNOWLEDGMENTS

We would like to express our sincere gratitude to:

Our husbands Paul and Whit for their love and belief that we are
capable of doing more than we ourselves envisioned.

Our children for their patience and encouragement even when
this project created personal inconveniences for them.

Justin Lee for his many hours proofing and typing.

Our parents Ronald and Dorothy Beach and O.B. and Edith Roberts for
modeling and teaching us what it means to be a person of good character.

Other school systems who were working on character
education and have shared ideas from their experiences.

The members of the Wake County School Board of Education who had the
conviction that character education was the right thing to do and took action.

Dr. Jim Surratt, Bill McNeal, and Sue King who have provided insightful leadership
and strong personal commitment to character education in Wake County.

The members of the Wake County Character Education Task Force for their
sensitivity to the needs of the community and their unselfish service.

The members of the Character Education Community Involvement
Committee for their continued passion for expanding character
development efforts throughout our community.

The many teachers who have enthusiastically embraced character
education and are creatively implementing it throughout the school day.

The wonderful parents who have encouraged us with
calls, letters, and personal involvement in the schools.

The numerous community leaders who have shared their time, effort and
even money to further the cause of character education in Wake County.

Mr. and Mrs. William F. Carl who generously sponsored a character forum for our community.

Dixon Smith and the staff at Character Development Group for
their patience, confidence in us, and professional expertise.

Phil Vincent for his personal encouragement and practical advice.

Thomas Lickona, Kevin Ryan and Rush Kidder for their wisdom, research, and resources.

The many individuals at Character Education Partnership, PREP,
and the Jefferson Center for sharing valuable information.

All the people who have prayed for and supported this effort.

God who has given us the opportunity to serve our
community and provided direction every step of the way.

Contents

THIS BOOK IS WRITTEN TO HELP
THOSE WHO WANT TO DEVELOP A
CHARACTER EDUCATION
PROGRAM. WE HOPE YOU WILL
FIND THE IDEAS PRESENTED
HELPFUL IN AFFECTING THE
CHARACTER DEVELOPMENT OF
THE CHILDREN IN YOUR
COMMUNITY. THE TASK IS
CHALLENGING BUT THE GOAL IS
VITAL FOR OUR FUTURE.

Introduction

Throughout the centuries, civic leaders have recognized that education entails more than simply providing students with knowledge and intellectual skills. Graduating students who can score extremely well on the SAT is an admirable goal, but it is a hollow victory if those students lack character. Who would want to hire them? Who would choose for their doctor an individual who earned straight A's but has no self-discipline concerning drugs or alcohol? Who would select a CPA who scored an 800 on the math portion of the SAT but has little integrity? These are the types of issues that schools must address. Character education is a good place to begin.

In the spring of 1997, the Wake County public school system in Raleigh, North Carolina, completed its third year of a comprehensive character education program. This book describes what we have learned from the process and offers readers suggestions to further their own efforts in the character development of students.

The Wake County public school system serves more than 85,000 students and employs more than 10,200 professional and support staff. It consists of more than 100 schools, making it the 33rd largest school system in the United States. Perhaps your school system is smaller, but the size or complexity of your school system does not matter. Consensus for character education can be reached in your community if the desire and commitment to succeed are present.

As you read this book, envision how character education can be accomplished in your community. It can! Take the ideas presented here and apply them in your specific situation. With careful adherence to the simple steps outlined in this book, you will be successful in your efforts.

We believe the process we used to develop community consensus and support for character education can be replicated successfully in any community. It also has application for initiatives other than character education. The basic ideas described in this book worked in Wake County and will work in your community as well.

Launching a new initiative is much like planning a journey. We will discuss possible destinations (goals and objectives), routes (processes and procedures), and necessary elements (people and concepts) for a successful trip. Take from our experience whatever ideas you like, and alter them to fit your specific situation.

One overriding concept must be emphasized at the outset: YOU can make a difference. Change begins with just one person or a small group of people. So often we feel overwhelmed by the magnitude of a problem and tend to accept defeat without even attempting to solve the problem. Yet history is filled with individuals and groups who changed its course armed solely with a good idea and the conviction and commitment to convert the idea into a reality.

The philosophy of the school room in one generation will be the philosophy of the government in the next.

Abraham Lincoln

Why The Need For Character Education

Character education is the central curriculum issue confronting educators. … it is a school's oldest mission.

During the past few decades, schools have experienced skyrocketing rates of crime, violence, drug and alcohol abuse, teen pregnancy, suspensions, and incidents revealing a lack of respect for others and responsibility for oneself. These are not strictly school problems but are reflective of our society at large. Communities are asking, "What is causing these problems, and what can we do about them?"

Although multiple causes have contributed to this situation, including the breakdown of the family, negative elements in the media, and racial prejudice, many educators are now looking at an even more fundamental cause — the erosion of character in our society.

Across the nation, schools are implementing character education as an integral part of the curriculum. Is this just another fad that will be loudly trumpeted today and disappear tomorrow?

Dr. Kevin Ryan, professor of education at Boston University and director of the university's Center for the Advancement of Ethics and Character, says, "Character education is the central curriculum issue confronting educators. Rather than the latest fad, it is a school's oldest mission."

Indeed, schools historically have considered the passing on of virtue and morality to the next generation an essential task. This was true from the early Greek academics through the first 300 years of our own country's educational institutions.

During the 1960s, however, our nation started losing sight of this goal. An increasing emphasis on individualism and individual rights, coupled with Supreme Court decisions that raised concerns about what schools could legally teach without crossing the line into religious instruction, led many educators to shy away from discussing morality and ethics with their students. Our schools were to be "value-free." References to God or religion were removed from many textbooks. "Values clarification" entered the school scene, with the teacher instructed not to convey any of his or her own concepts of right and wrong but to merely raise ethical questions and allow the students to determine their own values. (See page 15 for more information on values clarification.) Unfortunately, there was no yardstick of integrity or kindness or responsibility provided to help measure their ideas. Students too often have been left to believe that there are no basic rights and wrongs, yet our society is based on laws and values. Students often do not understand that, do not recognize basic rights and wrongs, and do not know how to apply ethical principles in their own day-to-day decision making.

Today we see the folly of a value-free approach to education. There is a massive movement in schools across our country to integrate character education into the curriculum. Does this mean that public schools are beginning to teach one religious point-of-view or taking a stand on volatile issues such as abortion and homosexuality? No. Character education is built on that common ground of values that all parents agree should be taught to children — those values that are esteemed by the major religions and civilized societies.

Character education in the public schools focuses on ethical principles such as responsibility, integrity, and respect. It is designed to complement the efforts of parents, the faith community and civic organizations in developing strong character.

Another factor contributing to the erosion of character among young people today is the lack of positive role models. Our nation has numerous celebrities but few heroes. Unfortunately this absence of strong role models reaches even into our classrooms and our homes. Many adults who have the opportunity to be a powerful force in positively influencing the character development of young people have abdicated that responsibility.

Also parents and teachers seem to be pointing the finger of blame at each other regarding less than desirable student behavior. Rather than considering one another teammates, working together to help children grow into good citizens, they each view the other as an adversary. Too often parents say teachers are unprofessional and teachers say parents are nonsupportive. Whereas parents used to appreciate a call from school and utilize this as an opportunity to teach their child responsibility for his or her own actions, the frequent response today is to defend the child and criticize the teacher. This trend must be reversed.

If character education efforts are to succeed, parents, teachers, and the extended community must once again recognize the need to work together in both teaching and modeling good character. The future of our children and our nation depend on it.

Many students today think any behavior is O.K. if they don't get caught.

For further information on the need for character education, we heartily recommend *Reclaiming Our Schools* by Edward Wynne and Kevin Ryan, and *Educating for Character: How Our Schools Can Teach Respect and Responsibility* by Thomas Lickona (see Resource Publications). Dr. Lickona has compiled "ten good reasons why schools should be making a clearheaded and wholehearted commitment to teaching moral values and developing good character." The following list summarizes Dr. Lickona's ten good reasons.

1. There is a clear and urgent need.
2. Transmitting values is and always has been the work of civilization.
3. The school's role as moral educator becomes even more vital at a time when millions of children get little moral teaching from their parents and value-centered influences such as church or temple are also absent from in their lives.
4. There is common ethical ground even in our value-conflicted society.
5. Democracies have a special need for moral education because democracy is government by the people themselves.
6. There is no such thing as value-free education.
7. The great questions facing both the individual and the human race are moral questions.
8. There is broad-based, growing support for values education in the schools.
9. An unabashed commitment to moral education is essential if we are to attract and keep good teachers.
10. Character education is a doable job.

The Four C's of Leadership

Each individual who desires to lead educators and communities in doing what is best for children must practice the Four C's of Leadership. These principles must be an integral part of every step you take and practiced by all the participants.

On page 32 you will find a set of worksheets which will help you with the specific steps required to initiate a character education program in your community. Throughout the process you will need to exercise conviction, commitment, communication and consensus-building.

1) CONVICTION

A conviction, not just in the head but also in the heart, is needed. Successful leaders are often described as having a genuine passion for their causes. A leader recognizes a need, has an idea for meeting that need, and a vision for how to set the process in motion.

This requires sharing one's conviction with others. The first group to convince that character education is the right thing to do is the school board. Unless its members are sold on the effort, success will not be achieved. They need to lead the charge, adopting a resolution of support for character education.

As soon as that is accomplished, several groups have to be engaged. School system administrators have to see the need and want to be active participants in the process. The principal at each school site is an extremely important key to the success of any program. Staff development needs to take place so that teachers can buy in to the concept and have input as to how it will be implemented. Parents must be contacted at the outset and

have opportunities to ask questions and to be actively involved. Conviction of the need for character education must continue to expand until it encompasses the community at large.

An example of the type of information that is helpful in convincing others is found on page 52. Other resource people and organizations are on page 46.

Ask yourself:
- What is character education?
- Does it really work?
- Why should our school system get involved with character education?

2) COMMITMENT

One must make the commitment to become personally involved in promoting character education. This will require time, energy, and the willingness to take a stand even when one may encounter some resistance. A leader must devote much time and effort to gathering information and formulating ideas from the many excellent resources available. One must view legitimate concerns and questions as opportunities to share this information. That is an essential part of the process of convincing others as outlined above so they will also commit themselves to the cause.

A concern that may arise is money. How much will a character education program cost? Unlike many new initiatives, it doesn't have to cost much. Character education can be integrated into the existing curriculum. Although additional supplemental materials may be added, the amount can be controlled by available funding. No new staff is required. Although some systems do select a person to

oversee the program, others give the responsibility to an existing staff member. Involving classroom teachers in developing curriculum ideas results in a product that is low-cost and tailor made to the community, while also promoting ownership on the part of the teachers.

Ask yourself:

- Am I willing to commit the time and effort needed to champion a character education program?
- What other individuals and groups are likely to be excited about this effort?
- What are the costs in time and energy as well as money?

3) COMMUNICATION

The next principle is to communicate the idea. Others must be made aware of the need, be convinced that the idea is a good one, commit to being involved, and go on to share the vision of what can be done. Research and enthusiasm are the keys to effective communication.

The first step in promoting a character education program is to collect data on local indications of the need. Newspaper articles, statistics from the judicial system, objective measures already available to your school board (i.e., major discipline problems, drug/alcohol/weapons violations, suspensions) as well as subjective observations can be helpful in documenting the need.

For general information and statistics from a national perspective, consider the chapter titled "The Case for Values Education" in Dr. Thomas Lickona's book *Educating for Character* (see Resource Publications). Dr.

Lickona cites ten "troubling youth trends," which he considers to be strong indicators that we are failing in our responsibility to provide for the moral development of our children:

1) Violence and vandalism
2) Stealing
3) Cheating
4) Disrespect for authority
5) Peer cruelty
6) Bigotry
7) Bad language
8) Sexual precocity and abuse
9) Increasing self-centeredness and declining civic responsibility
10) Self-destructive behavior

Begin the process of communicating the need for character education with the people closest to you and then expand the circle to include others. Parents and members of the school community — administrators, teachers, support staff, and students — are obvious targets for a communication campaign. Do not overlook other segments of the public, such as the faith community, business community and civic organizations, all of which can play a valuable role in supporting and implementing character education.

Ask yourself:

- Who is the key individual I need to approach first?
- What key group should be included to ensure the program's success?
- What information do I need to share with them?

4) CONSENSUS

The fourth principle is consensus-building. Character education is not an idea that should be pushed through over others' objections. In our experience, it should not be undertaken by mere majority rule but by consensus. The more attention given to encouraging widespread participation in the process and to careful consensus building, the more support your program will enjoy from the community at large. Individuals must have ample opportunity to ask questions, express concerns, and become part of the process. Special interest groups and their concerns must be identified and addressed. All segments of the community have to be invited to the table.

One must determine a common mission or goal that will unify the various segments of the community. Most school systems have a mission statement that incorporates the concept of character education. For example, Wake County's says it "will educate each student to be a responsible and productive citizen who can effectively manage future challenges." This mission clearly demands that behavioral and ethical concerns be addressed. *Ask yourself:*

· What issues may be divisive?
· What individuals or groups may be concerned about or even opposed to this effort?
· What theme or concept will encourage our community to work together?

Notes:

The direction in which education starts a man will determine his future life.

Plato

In some communities, the character education or values education movement has been met with suspicion and opposition due to fallout from the "values clarification" movement. Values clarification got its start in 1966 when New York University Professor Louis Raths wrote _Values and Teaching_. His thesis was that rather than giving students instruction in morality or ethics, the teacher should be a facilitator, assisting students in clarifying their own values.

According to Thomas Lickona, while values clarification may have encouraged students to think about what they valued and to be consistent in their actions, it tended to use the same approach for both trivial questions and important ethical issues, and it promoted moral relativism. Values clarification discussions failed to distinguish between what an individual might want to do (such as shoplift) and what an individual ought to do (respect the property rights of others). The approach did not require students to evaluate their own values against a standard and failed to suggest that some values might be better or worse than others. (Lickona, _Educating for Character_, p.11)

Due to these deficiencies, many educators and parents rejected values clarification. Because the term "values education" sounds similar to "values clarification" — although the process is totally different — most communities will respond more positively to the term "character education."

Creating a Community Task Force

Task force members must be open-minded, able to work with others, willing to listen, and committed to children and making a difference in their lives.

Once the decision has been made to proceed, the entire process of conviction, commitment, communication, and consensus-building must begin again with a group representing the community at large. This may be a large group called together in a summit or community forum, or it may be a smaller group such as a task force. Some districts use task forces, which, in turn, receive input from community focus groups. The important thing is that the group, regardless of its size or name, be carefully constructed to represent all the various segments of the community.

The necessity of building and maintaining avenues of communication with all areas of your community cannot be overemphasized. Otherwise groups left out of the process may attempt to derail the effort.

In forming a task force, it must include parents, teachers, principals, students and business, civic and religious leaders carefully selected to represent the various geographic areas, races, cultures and religions represented in your community. In order to prevent the task force from being too large, many of the members will need to represent more than one sector of the community.

Careful consideration must be given to the attributes of each potential task force member. Task force members must be open-minded, able to work with others, willing to listen, and committed to children and making a difference in their lives. It is also very important to have student representation on the task force and to solicit and respond to students' ideas. (See letter to the editor on p. 84.)

You may be pressured to place someone on the task force whom you feel does not exhibit the necessary qualities or who is motivated by a special interest. You may also be pressured to weight the task force heavily in a particular direction. It is essential that you not succumb to such pressures. Your goal is to form a task force that is truly representative of your entire community and composed of people capable of working together to achieve what is best for the students.

It is extremely important to choose the right chairperson. This individual should be knowledgeable, committed to character education, able to work well with people, and a consensus-builder.

As you plan the creation of a community task force, you need to anticipate potential pitfalls, roadblocks and detours, and map out a route to avoid them. Several documents are provided to act as a road map for the task force's journey. These documents, "Goals and

One example of a pitfall to be avoided is the word "tolerance." Several communities have found it to be a word that has different connotations to different people. To some, it is a beautiful word meaning freedom from prejudice or discrimination. To others, its derivation from the root word tolerate conveys a very low standard, i.e. "to put up with, to bear." Still others are concerned that tolerance could be construed as encouraging acceptance of all behaviors or lifestyles. In the interest of consensus-building it is recommended that other words, e.g., respect or caring, can be used to convey this important concept. If the task force members agree that the word tolerance should be used, it may be best to put it in the definition of one of these words.

Objectives," "Action Steps," "Guidelines," "Ground Rules" and "Working Definitions" are found on pages 18-21.

After deciding whom you wish to serve on the task force, an invitation from the school board should be sent to each person selected. A sample invitation is provided below. You may want to make the first meeting a dinner function to indicate the value your school system places on the task force and its mission.

The following is a sample invitation that might be sent to prospective task force members:

> "We must remember that education is not enough. **Intelligence** plus **character** — that is the true goal of education."
>
> The Rev. Martin Luther King, Jr.

...form a task force that is truly representative of your entire community and composed of people capable of working together to achieve what is best for the students.

Sample letter to potential task force members:

> *Each day we are faced with news stories documenting the increase in violence in our society and the apparent decline in basic human values among some of our young people. For many of us, such problems are not confined to the newspaper columns and TV broadcasts. They have intruded upon our streets, places of work, homes, and even our schools. We all have heard reports of fights, weapons and thefts in schools; widespread alcohol, drug and tobacco use among school children; escalating teenage pregnancy rates; and teachers abandoning the profession out of frustration and sometimes fear.*
>
> *Although many young people continue to do well and our school staffs work very hard to provide positive, caring, learning environments for our children, we need to do all we can to support our students by instilling in them a strong sense of personal responsibility. We need to convey to our children high expectations regarding not only academic performance but also character development.*
>
> *Based on this need, the _____ Board of Education requests that you consider participating in a task force on character education, which will be headed by _____. As a member of the task force, you will be working with _____ of your fellow citizens as we attempt to identify the character traits that are important to our citizenry and determine how these traits can best be taught to youth. Our first meeting will be _____. Please call _____ by _____ to indicate whether you will be willing and able to serve on this important committee.*

Laying the Groundwork for a Successful Task Force

The task force's primary purpose is to identify those concepts that all agree should be taught to children — those concepts esteemed by the major religions and civilized societies. In order to achieve that purpose, members of the task force must share the same goal and objectives. Therefore, prior to the first meeting of the task force its goal, objectives and the means of achieving them should be established. The following documents were distributed to Wake County's task force:

GOAL

To counter influences promoting school violence, disrespect for authority, selfishness, dishonesty and lack of discipline by establishing a program of character education for the Wake County public school system focused positively on broad-based traits of good behavior.

OBJECTIVES

- To affirm and support the character goals of families who send their children to our schools by providing instruction on broadly supported traits of good character and affirming their practice.
- To develop an atmosphere in our public schools that considers good character something worthy of praise.
- To help children attending our schools to learn to think before they act, to understand fundamental differences between right and wrong, and to make good decisions.
- To help children attending our schools to understand better what their community expects of them in terms of good character.
- To put our school system in a leadership

position demonstrating to others how broadly based principles of good character can be taught in the public school setting.

With a clear goal and objectives the destination of the journey is established. The next step is to identify the route to that destination. Devising a series of action steps is a good way to get moving.

ACTION STEPS

- Establish procedures for determining character traits that can be supported and enhanced collaboratively by the schools, parents, and entire community.
- Share the list of character traits with school staffs, parents, students, where appropriate, and the entire community.
- Receive input from all groups to determine additions, deletions, and/or priorities.
- Compile input from all groups and present final character traits list to the Board of Education.
- Publish and disseminate the list to all groups.
- Refer character traits list to the school system staff to develop a plan for incorporating the traits into the curriculum.
- Review the completed plan with the Character Education Task Force.
- Share the character education curriculum plan with school staffs, parents, students, where appropriate, and the entire community.
- Receive input from all groups.
- Compile input from all groups and present the final plan to the Board of Education.

In order to clarify the route, the following

It should be emphasized that the goal is to find "common ground" that the entire community will support.

guidelines can be distributed to the task force. It should be emphasized that the goal is to find common ground that the entire community will support. Also, task force members need to keep in mind that the objective of a character education program is to complement the efforts of parents and the faith community in developing strong character, not to teach one religious point of view or to take a stand on volatile public issues.

GUIDELINES

1. Focus will be on developing a limited list of core character traits. This means the list will not be exhaustive and will not include all worthy possibilities. A final list of more than five but fewer than ten is desirable.

2. Traits included must be generally supported by the task force members and should be perceived as broadly held throughout the community.

- Traits that become controversial will be disqualified from further consideration.
- No trait that is unique to one religious or non-religious moral tradition and that is unacceptable to others will be included. Any trait that cannot be supported broadly will not be included.

3. Because the framework for a character education curriculum is intended for use in the public schools, it will respect, but will not include, instruction on religious reasons for developing good character. A discussion of the nature of ultimate moral authority will not be included.

4. The task force will view its work as an effort to affirm and support the character goals of families who send their children to our schools. This means the task force will take care to ensure its work does not preempt or

supplant the role of families in shaping the character of their children.

The task force action steps and guidelines lay the foundation for developing consensus. The action steps outline a process for soliciting comment from all segments of the community. The guidelines define the trait selection process in such a way as to preclude its disintegration into controversy or partisan bickering. There is one other document that the task force will find useful in consensus-building. The "Suggested Ground Rules," listed below, provide a blueprint for how the task force should operate. In Wake County, the ground rules were an invaluable tool for keeping each participant focused on the fact that we, as task force members, needed to display those very character traits that we desired to teach our children. You may want to consider having your task force briefly review the ground rules at the start of each meeting throughout the process of selecting and defining the character traits.

SUGGESTED GROUND RULES

We are all equal. Rules of civility begin with us.

- Task force members will be expected to work for consensus, resulting in a product that will have the support of our community.
- Each member will have an opportunity to speak on every issue but not monopolize the discussion.
- Task force members should feel free to express their convictions and concerns but always with a spirit of congeniality and respect.
- All points of view will be listened to

We are all equal. Rules of civility begin with us.

Of all the properties which belong to honorable men, not one is so highly prized as that of character.

Henry Clay

respectfully.

- If the meeting becomes unproductive for any person, he or she should express this concern to the group.
- Task force meetings will be open to the public.
- The chairperson is the spokesperson for the task force. Any major concerns should be shared directly with the task force chairperson.

Before beginning to actually identify the core character traits, the task force should consider establishing definitions of key words. The following definitions may facilitate your process.

CHARACTER:

- those attributes indicative of an individual's ethical strength
- moral excellence
- the way you act when no one is looking

CHARACTER TRAITS: *the inner qualities of an individual that are exemplified in behaviors or incline the will to choose right over wrong*

It is extremely important to convey to the task force and to the community at large the differences among character traits, behaviors, and issues. A character trait is a heart attitude or a guiding principle that affects numerous behaviors. It would be impossible to list all the specific behaviors one might wish children to display. It would be even more difficult, perhaps impossible, to reach agreement on

specific desirable behaviors within a diverse community. For example, many parents may want their children to establish eye contact when adults are speaking to them, but in some cultures this would be considered very rude since children are expected to lower their eyes when addressed by adults. The character trait "respect," however, encompasses both behaviors.

Some people may be concerned that a character education program is going to deal with controversial issues. They may fear that there is a hidden agenda regarding such issues as abortion, homosexuality or euthanasia, or that a particular religious or political point-of-view will be presented as more desirable than others. It is essential that all parties realize that character education focuses on the development of those inner qualities, such as responsibility, integrity, and kindness, that are esteemed by all people. It does not promote a particular position on controversial issues that may divide the community.

CONSENSUS: *everyone agrees to support the decision*

The definition of consensus is constructed to emphasize the desirability of unanimous support for the end product. Making decisions by consensus encourages task force members to engage in respectful discussion in a spirit of cooperation, not competition. Rather than pitting participants against one another in a debate format to obtain a few more votes, it establishes an atmosphere of congenial discussion to discover those ideas the entire group values. It also provides protection against the final document being the product of a dominant group whose opinions differ markedly from those of other members.

Consensus does not mean that 100 percent agreement is necessary for every decision because requiring unanimity leaves open the possibility that one person could hold the entire process hostage to his or her personal agenda. However, it should be understood that the goal is to develop a product that everyone on the task force can enthusiastically support.

You should be prepared for the possibility that not everyone will wish to seek consensus. Perhaps a story such as the one below can help move people away from gridlock:

Once there was a very wise king. People from far and near would come to him to resolve their conflicts for they knew him to be of great discernment in his judgments. One day two women came before the king, each claiming the same child to be her son. After hearing the accounts, the king asked for a sword. He then decreed that the child would be divided in two, with each woman receiving one-half. One woman agreed with this judgment, but the other woman fervently appealed to the king not to kill the child but to give him instead to her rival. Then the king responded, "Do not cut the child in half. Give him to the one who was willing to let him go; she is the true mother." (paraphrased from I Kings 3:16-28)

Discuss the story's relevance to the operation of the task force. It is hoped that such a discussion will demonstrate that those who truly desire what is best for the children will be less interested in personal ownership of the specific words selected and more concerned with the overall goal of identifying those basic concepts that will best benefit the children.

Notes:

_____

_____

_____

_____

_____

_____

_____

_____

_____

_____

_____

_____

_____

_____

_____

_____

_____

_____

_____

_____

_____

_____

_____

_____

_____

The task force's primary purpose is to identify those concepts that all agree should be taught to children…

Identifying and Defining the Character Traits

Over a period of several weeks and maybe months, the task force will undertake the process of selecting the traits that should be the foundation of the school district's character education program. Have the members begin with a brainstorming session designed to identify possible traits. Lists of traits identified by other school districts that have developed character education programs may be shared with the task force, if desired.

During an initial brainstorming session, the Wake County task force suggested more than 60 different traits, all of which were recorded on large sheets of paper taped to the wall. Each participant was given ten adhesive dots and asked to place them by his or her top ten choices. The list was then narrowed down by the following means:

- elimination of traits with no votes
- elimination of traits with few votes
- combining words that addressed the same concepts and choosing the word that best represented the concept (e.g., "honest" and "trustworthy" both became part of the definition of the trait identified as "integrity")
- elimination of words that didn't fit the definition of character trait (e.g., "community involvement" was eliminated because it was a behavior, not a character trait, but was included in the definition of "responsibility")
- transference of words that conveyed a narrow aspect of a broader concept, often with a recommendation that the word be incorporated into the definition of the trait (e.g., "considerate," "courteous," and "helpful" were included within the broader concept "kindness")

Once the list of character traits is determined, the task force must agree upon definitions of the terms. One way to begin is with dictionary definitions. The task force can then delete from or add to those definitions. The task force can be divided into groups, with each group assigned the task of defining one trait. Another way to proceed is to ask for volunteers for a small subcommittee to write a rough draft of the definitions. The entire task force can then respond to the draft.

The following are the definitions developed by the Wake County Task Force for their eight character traits.

CHARACTER TRAITS

COURAGE — Having the determination to do the right thing even when others don't; the strength to follow your conscience rather than the crowd. Attempting difficult things that are worthwhile.

GOOD JUDGMENT — Choosing worthy goals and setting proper priorities. Thinking through the consequences of your actions. Basing decisions on practical wisdom and good sense.

INTEGRITY — Having the inner strength to be truthful, trustworthy, and honest in all things. Acting justly and honorably.

KINDNESS — Being considerate, courteous, helpful, and understanding of others. Showing care, compassion, friendship, and generosity. Treating others as you would like to be treated.

PERSEVERANCE — Being persistent in pursuit of worthy objectives in spite of difficulty, opposition, or discouragement. Exhibiting patience and having the fortitude to try again when confronted with delays, mistakes, or failures.

RESPECT — Showing high regard for authority, for other people, for self, for property, and for country. Understanding that all people have value as human beings.

RESPONSIBILITY — Being dependable in carrying out obligations and duties. Showing reliability and consistency in words and conduct. Being accountable for your own actions. Being committed to active involvement in your community.

SELF-DISCIPLINE — Demonstrating hard work and commitment to purpose. Regulating yourself for improvement and refraining from inappropriate behaviors. Being in proper control of your words, actions, impulses, and desires. Choosing abstinence from premarital sex, drugs, alcohol, tobacco, and other harmful substances and behaviors. Doing your best in all situations.

The Josephson Institute's Six Pillars of Character

- TRUSTWORTHINESS: honesty, integrity, promise-keeping, loyalty
- RESPECT: autonomy, privacy, dignity, courtesy, tolerance, acceptance
- RESPONSIBILITY: accountability, pursuit of excellence
- CARING: compassion, consideration, giving, sharing, kindness, loving
- JUSTICE & FAIRNESS: procedural fairness, impartiality, consistency, equality, equity, due process
- CIVIC VIRTUE & CITIZENSHIP: law abiding, community service, protection of environment

The National School Boards Association List

- altruism
- compassion
- courage
- courtesy
- generosity
- honesty
- industriousness
- integrity
- loyalty
- obedience
- punctuality
- respect for authority
- responsibility
- self-discipline
- self-respect
- tolerance

Some systems have begun the trait selection process in a slightly different way. They have asked smaller groups to brainstorm possible character traits and then select their top five choices. Sometimes these groups are simply subcommittees of the task force; sometimes they are community focus groups held at various places throughout the school district. Each group then shares its list with the entire task force and the process continues as above.

Still other communities have gathered lists of traits from other communities or organizations and have worked from these. Beginning with lists devised by another group will expedite the process but may dilute the richness that occurs with a "start from scratch" approach. Another group's list, however, can provide a foundation on which to begin building. Both approaches are acceptable and can lead to successful programs. You must determine which would be most suitable for your community.

After the Character Traits Are Determined and Defined

Surveying the community

After the task force has agreed upon the character traits and their definitions, the next step is to assess the degree of support within the community for implementing a character education program designed to teach those traits. Survey forms can be sent home with all students and made available for interested citizens to pick up at all schools and public libraries. In addition, some students can be surveyed. For example, the task force might decide to ask students in grades 4, 7, and 10 to respond. Local newspapers should also be asked to publish the survey. A copy of a possible survey is on page 49, followed by additional information regarding Wake County's survey.

The survey should ask respondents whether they agree with the teaching of each individual character trait. In addition, respondents should be encouraged to write comments, either in space provided on the survey form or on separate sheets.

After the surveys have been collected, the task force can develop tables or graphs showing the percentage of respondents in favor of teaching each trait. All written comments should be read, and common concerns can be grouped together and discussed in a summary of the survey findings. The results of the survey need to be shared with the community. There is a great deal of interest in and support for the

teaching of character traits in the schools. It is hoped that your community survey will demonstrate that fact.

Developing a brochure

Next, a group within the task force must begin working on a brochure to explain the goals of character education, summarize the task force's work thus far, report the survey results, and answer frequently asked questions. This is an excellent way to educate the community about the program and to increase community support. Questions and concerns raised by survey respondents can be addressed in the brochure. Wake County's brochure is printed on pages 52-55 and the Nash-Rocky Mount, North Carolina, Schools' brochure is printed on pages 56-57 to provide examples and also to suggest succinct answers to some of the most frequently asked questions.

As with the surveys, brochures can be sent home with students and should be made available at all schools and public libraries. For even wider dissemination, the task force can ask local stores to make brochures available and can request that local newspapers print it.

Enlisting the support of the entire community

The job of developing, encouraging and affirming good character can be compared to a three-legged stool. The child sits on this "seat

Letters Regarding Wake County's Character Education Survey

■ Overall Supportive 61.8%

▨ Overall Critical 26.6%

▨ Undecided/Not Clear 11.5%

of character," trusting that it will provide secure support. Traditionally the support for this stool has been the three strong "legs" of the home, the school, and the community, especially the faith community. If any one of these legs does not provide proper support, the stool will tilt, possibly even fall, injuring the child in the process.

Through the survey and brochure, many members of the community will be made aware of the need for character education and become supporters of the program. The process of enlisting community support, however, is an ongoing one, and it is critical that all segments of the community be reminded of their role in supporting character development. Following are some brief descriptions of how parents, businesses, the community at large, and the media can support the development of character.

Many of these suggestions resulted from a Community Character Forum held in Wake County in October 1996. For a complete listing of action ideas resulting from that forum, see page 72.

Role of parents

As Wake County's character education brochure states, "Parents have the primary responsibility for their child's education in moral character." The school's role is to reinforce and support the efforts of parents as models and teachers of good character. In order to accomplish this, a school system can, among other things, provide speakers for PTA/PTO programs or parent coffees, offer parent workshops on issues related to effective parenting and discipline, work with other organizations on integrating the language of

character into their parenting programs, and encourage the faith community to focus on character in parenting classes, Sunday school classes and outreach ministries. The schools can also make available to parents the list of "25 Suggestions for Parents," which is reproduced on page 66.

Role of the business community

The business community readily sees the importance of character development. Employers are genuinely concerned about the "character fitness" of future employees and their ability to make ethical decisions in the workplace. They desire to have employees who will come to work on time, get along with others, and conduct themselves with integrity. We have found the business community eager to support character education efforts with both time and money. For example, a local business organization can establish Community Service Awards to recognize and reward citizenship, leadership, service and exemplary character. Employers can provide ethics training and encourage and affirm displays of good character by their employees. Business leaders can visit schools to share their personal "character stories" with students or provide employees with paid release time to spend one-half day a month working with children in the schools. Businesses can also highlight the importance of character in ads or billboards.

Role of the community at large

Children spend much of their time interacting with people in the community. Many children attend religious services or religious education programs. Large numbers

of children participate in community-sponsored sports activities and organizations like the scouts. Each of these groups has a role to play in helping shape the character of the children involved in its activities.

Members of the clergy can devote time in sermons or children's programs to discussing the relationship among morals, character and behavior. The faith community can sponsor parent discussion groups or parenting classes, recognize students who display good character and pray for character development in children and the community.

The coaches of sports teams can emphasize character traits and teach children how to both win and lose graciously. Civic and community organizations can provide service opportunities for children, such as crop walks, food banks or neighborhood cleanup projects; establish Community Service Awards; adopt schools and provide mentors and tutors for the students at those schools; and design "Help Your Neighbor" community projects that emphasize character traits.

Role of the media

The media can be a powerful ally in getting your message out to the community. It is essential to develop good relationships with media representatives, provide them with well-prepared, up-to-date information, and keep the lines of communication open.

In Wake County, we were fortunate to get the cooperation of three local television stations. The local ABC affiliate aired several news stories on the character education program, traveling to different schools and interviewing teachers and students. The local CBS affiliate filmed some delightful public service announcements on several of our character traits, utilizing local children. The reaction of the community to those spots was most enthusiastic. The CBS station also involved us in a call-in program focused on child-related issues and followed that with a public affairs program on character education. The local WB affiliate also filmed and aired several public service announcements on each of our character traits. These were designed to appeal to younger viewers and were aired during children's programming.

We continue to provide the media with fresh information about our character education program. An article in our school system newsletter requesting stories about people of character along with a sample news release is on page 71.

In Wake County we decided to develop a logo which would convey the importance of character development. Our award-winning poster, which is displayed throughout our community, was a success in creating an identity for the character education program.

Survey comments:

- "I think this program is definitely needed for our children. It is increasingly difficult to teach morals to children in today's society.... I am 100 percent in favor of positive character development being taught in schools." *(Parent)*

- "I fully endorse this endeavor. I'm sorry that this responsibility is falling on the school system. However, if we care about our future, we cannot afford to sit on the sidelines and say, 'It's not my job.'" *(Parent)*

- "All of the qualities listed on the survey sheet are unquestionably essential, however they must be taught at home." *(Teacher)*

- 'Thank you for this survey. It is very important for students to have input on decisions in the classroom." *(Fourth grader)*

- "I am personally all for what the program will accomplish. This program can never take the place of good parenting, but it can prevent the most serious structural damage to the foundation of our children, their morality." *(Tenth grader)*

- We do not offend any of the diverse religious groups found in Wake County, or those belonging to no religion, by teaching such character traits." *(Parent)*

- "I think you would be better off giving character classes to parents." *(Parent)*

- Given an opportunity for discussion, I might quibble over a few points. But taken as a whole, I can support this list as a basis for teaching positive character attributes to my children and their classmates." *(Parent)*

- "I applaud the work done by the Character Education Task Force. I feel that your efforts have been well directed, and your list of traits comprehensive and well reasoned." *(Community member)*

- "Teaching character isn't something you teach from a book it is something you teach by example." *(Parent)*

- "If I thought for one minute a school I had my kids in did not automatically stress these values, I would pull my kids from that school immediately." *(Parent)*

- "I am worried about an extra burden being placed on educators." *(Teacher)*

"To educate a person in mind and not in morals is to educate a menace to society."

Theodore Roosevelt

Towards Implementation: The Role of the Schools

One should be very skeptical about buying a curriculum that by itself promises to develop character in youth.

Once the character education program is designed, attention must be turned to implementation. To oversee this part of the process, as well as to keep the momentum going, a character education advocate should be selected. This person will be responsible for facilitating the implementation of character education within the schools.

First, school personnel must receive training. There are consultants and training groups who work with schools and communities to provide such training. To be successful, the training must be consistent throughout the entire system and must emphasize that character education is not just another "add-on" program for the schools. A word of caution: One should be very skeptical about buying a curriculum that promises to develop character in youth. It will not work without commitment from school staffs and opportunities for the staffs to develop ownership in the process. (See related materials on pp.62- 65.)

We also recommend that character education be a K-12 initiative and that no school be excused from the effort. The need is well documented and time too short to begin with a pilot project. A system wide program is also an indication of the value you place on this initiative.

Character education must become part of the "ethos" or life of the school. It must represent what we are all about. The goal should be to integrate character education into all areas of the curriculum, permeate the school climate with support for and encouragement of character, and sustain and expand community involvement in the process. The sections below briefly discuss the three key aspects of the successful character education program: curriculum, school climate, and community involvement.

The curriculum

Character education is not a separate course to be added to the curriculum. Rather it must be integrated into the entire curriculum.

It is evident that many subject areas are well-suited to discussions of character. Language arts courses, for example, are rich with opportunities for talking about the elements of character and analyzing whether individuals in a story displayed a particular trait. Students can infer how a story might have changed if a character had exhibited kindness or courage or perseverance. They can select which character they admire the most or would like to have as a friend and tell why. Journal and creative writing offer limitless opportunities for focusing on issues of character.

History and social studies also afford tremendous possibilities for highlighting character. Individuals and events can be examined for evidence of how commitment to a particular character trait may have altered history itself. How can events such as the Holocaust or the civil rights movement be studied without reference to the importance of respect for others?

In science classes, the importance of integrity in research might be discussed. In physical education, a teacher might emphasize the necessity of self-discipline and perseverance. In theater arts, an ethical dilemma might be presented, and students could be instructed to improvise a way to resolve the situation.

The ideas are never-ending.

Educators must identify where character education already exists and additional areas where it can easily be incorporate into the existing curriculum. Many teachers already emphasize character, but we need a more organized effort to incorporate the language of character throughout the curriculum and to take advantage of those teachable moments.

School climate

The second area of focus must be the school climate. The goal is to create a culture of character in our schools. We want to reverse the current trend in which it is considered "cool" to break the rules and get away with it. Our goal is to model and affirm ethical behavior so that it is once again considered cool to be a person of character.

Whenever modeling is mentioned there are always a few people who say, "I don't want to be a role model. I was hired to teach, not to be a role model." How do you respond to that?

The question is not "Do you want to be a role model?" All of us are role models whether we want to be or not. Our students are constantly watching our attitudes and behaviors. The question is whether you will be a positive or negative role model. We can discuss elements of character with our students all day long, but if we don't display those same character traits, our words will be totally void. (See letter from parent on p. 69.) Someone once said, "The footsteps children most often follow are those we thought we'd covered up."

Educators need to assess the climate at their schools to determine how well it encourages and affirms the practice of good charac-

ter. The behavior code and discipline policies should be carefully examined. A sense of community and pride in "our school" should be promoted.

Community involvement

The third focus area for character education is community involvement. Traditionally, the home, the schools, and the faith community were seen as partners in training children to be good citizens. Somewhere along the way, we lost that cooperative spirit and replaced it with a suspicious, critical, and sometimes even adversarial relationship. Our goal is to recapture the idea that we are all on the same team, working toward a common goal.

Schools need to welcome members of the community as volunteers and use them effectively. Tutors and mentors can play a significant role in character development. During a time when many children lack positive role models or adults who display a keen personal interest in them, a committed tutor or mentor can be life-changing. Community members can also be utilized as motivational speakers and readers. Examples of how one elementary school used volunteers in character education is found on page 54.

Just as the community needs to come into the schools, the schools need to go into the community. More and more school systems are recognizing the value of giving students opportunities to serve their community. Dr. Thomas Lickona says students not only have to "know the good," they have to also "desire the good" and then "do the good." They need to put into practice those character traits they are being taught and to experience the

"A teacher can't establish classroom rules, relate to kids, or discuss a piece of literature without communicating values."

Henry A. Huffman

... to truly learn to care, ...students must become involved in service toward others.

Philip Vincent

intangible rewards that come from helping others. The possibilities are endless, from cleaning up the environment to working at a food bank, from visiting hospitalized children to having "buddies" at a nursing home. A newspaper article describing a community service project undertaken by students from a middle school in Wake County is on page 83.

You need to continue promoting ever-expanding community involvement through the same process by which you began — the four C's discussed at the beginning of this workbook. As others acquire the conviction of the importance of character education, they will develop a commitment to become part of the process and a desire to communicate the vision to others, resulting in consensus and owner-ship throughout the community.

Notes:

Watch your thoughts;
    they become words.
Watch your words;
    they become actions.
Watch your actions;
    they become habits.
Watch your habits;
    they become character.
Watch your character;
    it becomes your destiny.

Frank Outlaw

Conclusion

The actual process of character development is a never-ending journey. It is a crucial journey for each of us, not just the students but every adult in the community. Those who desire to effectively teach young people to practice good habits of character must demonstrate them. Each one who becomes committed to this process will become keenly aware of his/her own shortcomings and must purpose to be a more consistent role model.

We may never get to the point in our journey where we can say we've arrived. Detractors may point to the fact that problems still exist in our schools. Yet we should be extremely encouraged by the progress being made. Personal anecdotes, which we in Wake County continually receive from teachers, parents, students, and community members, should keep us excitedly moving forward. Two examples are shared here.

From a high school secretary: Immediately following spring break, a student brought a note from her mother indicating that she had missed the two days prior to vacation due to illness. Several days later the mother herself came in, asking to speak to the person in charge of attendance. She indicated that her daughter had been writing a paper on the importance of integrity and both mother and daughter began feeling guilty. It seems that the absence had been due to a family vacation rather than illness. They made the decision to set the record straight.

From a fifth grade teacher: Upon entering the classroom each morning, my students write in their journals. The journal entries can be about any topic they wish, and are seen only be me.

One of my students was a young man named James. He has been well known since entering school for having a quick temper and even faster fists. Although James has heard many lessons on the eight character traits, I was not sure how much was really sinking in.

One day I was so impressed with James' journal entry that I asked for and received his permission to share it with the entire class.

"This morning I got off the bus and came down the hall and Matt hit me and ran away. Last year when I was younger I would have gone after him and hit him so hard that he wouldn't ever do that anymore. But now I'm a responsible fifth grader and I know sometimes it takes more courage not to fight than to fight so I used my self-discipline and just kept on walking!"

The entire class stood and applauded.

The journey into character education is not easy. It requires a clear vision of one's destination, careful planning of the route, continued commitment along the way, and time. We hope that our "travelogue" has provided you with information to aid you in your journey. Have a wonderful trip!

The Worksheets

The prospect of initiating any new program in a school system can seem somewhat overwhelming. There are so many ideas to keep in mind and details to remember. The enormity of the task can be rather intimidating. It reminds us of the children's riddle:

Question: How do you eat an elephant?

Answer: One bite at a time.

The obvious parallel here is that you must break down the task of developing a character education program into "bite-sized" pieces. This section of the book is designed to help you do just that. Each page guides you through a step in the process of initiating a character education program. We hope you'll find them helpful.

Remember, take one step at a time and enjoy the walk through the steps.

STEPS TO CONSENSUS ON CHARACTER EDUCATION

STEP 1

Identify and document the need in your community for addressing issues of character. (Related text on pp. 10-13.)

1. What behavioral concerns are being expressed by teachers? By parents?

2. What information can be gleaned from school or community statistics? (suspensions, dropouts, teen pregnancies, alcohol and drug violations, weapons, office referrals for discipline, community crime statistics involving juveniles, etc.)

STEP 2

Research character education as a possible solution.(Related text on pp. 10-11 and resources on p. 46)

1.   What is character education?

_____
_____
_____
_____
_____
_____
_____
_____
_____
_____
_____
_____
_____

2.   Where are there effective programs that should be examined as resources?

_____
_____
_____
_____
_____
_____
_____
_____
_____
_____
_____
_____
_____
_____
_____

3.   What elements do those programs have in common?

_____
_____
_____
_____
_____
_____
_____
_____
_____
_____
_____

4.   Collect data regarding the effectiveness of other programs.

_____
_____
_____
_____
_____
_____
_____
_____
_____
_____
_____
_____
_____
_____
_____
_____
_____
_____
_____

STEP 3

Develop a heartfelt conviction that character education is the right thing to do.

Write a statement expressing why you want to initiate a character education program and what you hope to accomplish.

Successful leaders have a genuine passion for their causes.

STEP 4

Make the commitment to follow through.
(Related text pp. 12-14)

1. Who needs to be involved in the process?

2. What are the costs in time and energy as well as money?

3. Determine your personal commitment to this process, outlining goals, action steps, and target dates for completion.

One must make the committment to become personally involved in promoting character education.

STEP 5

Communicate your vision to others.

1. Who is the key individual that you need to approach first?

   _____

   _____

   _____

2. List three or four reasons for character education that will appeal to that person.

   _____

   _____

   _____

   _____

   _____

   _____

   _____

   _____

   _____

   _____

3. What is the key group that needs to be involved to ensure the program's success?

   _____

   _____

   _____

4. When and how can you present your vision to them?

   _____

   _____

   _____

   _____

   _____

   _____

   _____

_____

_____

_____

_____

_____

_____

5. Outline your presentation below. What handouts or overheads will support your case?

   _____

   _____

   _____

   _____

   _____

   _____

   _____

   _____

   _____

   _____

   _____

   _____

   _____

   _____

   _____

   _____

   _____

STEP 6

Assess the specific characteristics of your community.

1. What issues may be divisive?

_____

_____

_____

_____

_____

_____

_____

_____

_____

2. What groups may have concerns or even be opposed to this effort?

_____

_____

_____

_____

_____

_____

_____

_____

3. Who are key individuals or organizations that need to be briefed in order to solicit their support? (educational groups, the media, etc.)

_____

_____

_____

_____

_____

_____

_____

_____

_____

_____

_____

4. Identify:
    *   special interest groups
    *   geographic areas
    *   faith communities
    *   races and ethnic groups
    *   other groups that need to be involved in the process

_____

_____

_____

_____

_____

_____

_____

_____

_____

_____

_____

_____

_____

_____

_____

_____

_____

_____

_____

_____

_____

_____

_____

_____

_____

_____

_____

_____

_____

_____

STEP 7

Identify specific strategies and procedures for reaching consensus.

Select a small core group to brainstorm questions such as:

1. How will consensus be defined?

_____

_____

_____

_____

_____

2. What processes and procedures will be needed?

_____

_____

_____

_____

_____

_____

_____

_____

_____

_____

_____

_____

_____

_____

_____

_____

3. Do we need an official vote or "charge" from a board or individual? If so, how will we proceed in securing that objective?

_____

_____

_____

_____

_____

_____

_____

_____

_____

_____

4. What will be our time frame?

_____

_____

_____

_____

_____

_____

_____

5. What theme or concept will encourage our community to work together?

_____

_____

_____

_____

_____

_____

_____

STEP 8

Set up a task force. (Related text pp. 16-17)

1. Identify individuals to represent each of the groups listed in Step #6.

_____
_____
_____
_____
_____
_____
_____
_____
_____
_____
_____
_____
_____
_____
_____
_____
_____
_____
_____
_____
_____
_____
_____
_____
_____
_____
_____
_____
_____
_____

2. Decide how final selection will be determined? (interview, letter, nomination by group, etc.)

_____
_____
_____
_____
_____
_____
_____
_____
_____
_____
_____

3. List the qualities desired in a chairperson and prospective names. Make a final selection prior to the first meeting of the task force.

_____
_____
_____
_____
_____
_____
_____
_____
_____
_____
_____
_____
_____
_____
_____

STEP 9

Select the traits and define them. (Related text pp. 18-23)

Describe the process the task force will use in trait selection.

1. How will the task force be made aware of certain "hot button" words?

_____

_____

_____

_____

_____

_____

_____

2. Will you share lists from other school systems or other programs? Why or why not?

_____

_____

_____

_____

_____

_____

_____

_____

_____

3. Determine the process for defining the traits.

_____

_____

_____

_____

_____

_____

_____

_____

_____

STEP 10

Establish a means for involving the community at large in reaching consensus on what should be taught.

1. How will you get input from the community? (survey, focus groups at each school, community forums, etc.)

3. How will the traits and definitions be finalized and adopted by the community?

2. How will community opinion be gathered and tallied?

STEP 11

Implement the program. (Related text pp. 24-30)

1. Who will be responsible? Will the same person be the "character education advocate"?

_____

_____

_____

_____

_____

2. Who is responsible for implementation at the various levels (i.e., each curriculum area, school site)?

_____

_____

_____

_____

_____

_____

_____

_____

_____

3. What groups will be involved and how?

_____

_____

_____

_____

_____

_____

_____

_____

_____

_____

_____

4. What staff development needs to take place?

_____

_____

_____

_____

_____

_____

_____

_____

_____

_____

_____

_____

5. Will you purchase a prepared curriculum or design your own?

_____

_____

6. What additional materials will be needed?

_____

_____

_____

_____

_____

_____

_____

_____

_____

STEP 12

Develop and maintain ever-broadening community involvement.

1. What specific measures will be used to involve:
   the home?
   the faith community?
   the civic and business community?
   other individuals and groups who work with children?

   _____
   _____
   _____
   _____
   _____
   _____
   _____
   _____
   _____
   _____
   _____
   _____
   _____
   _____
   _____
   _____

2. Will all or any of the task force members have an ongoing role? What will it be?

   _____
   _____
   _____
   _____
   _____
   _____
   _____
   _____
   _____
   _____

3. What measures will be used to continue encouraging two-way communication between the schools and the community?

   _____
   _____
   _____
   _____
   _____
   _____
   _____
   _____
   _____
   _____
   _____
   _____
   _____

4. What additional groups or individuals need to be involved?

   _____
   _____
   _____
   _____
   _____
   _____
   _____
   _____
   _____
   _____

5. In what additional ways can the media assist in the process?

   _____
   _____
   _____
   _____
   _____
   _____
   _____

BIOGRAPHIES

J

u d y   B .   H o f f m a n

Judy Hoffman has dedicated her life to the needs of children and education. A native of Michigan, Mrs. Hoffman earned a B.M. ed., with a minor in math, from the University of Michigan. She began her career in education as a teacher in Montgomery County, Maryland. In 1978, she and her family relocated to Raleigh, North Carolina.

As a foster parent and the mother of four children, Mrs. Hoffman has witnessed firsthand the need for leadership and daily involvement in educational and children's issues. She has juggled active memberships on three PTAs and served as chairman of an area high school advisory council. Mrs. Hoffman also founded the organization, Advocate Citizens for Education.

She serves on the executive committee of the North Carolina Partnership for Children, the board of directors of Wake County Smart Start, the education committee of the Greater Raleigh Chamber of Commerce, the Tammy Lynn Center and has previously served on the boards of Communities in Schools and Wake Education Partnerships. Among her other contributions is the founding of the toy and equipment lending library at the Tammy Lynn Center.

Her most visible role, however, was that of chairman of the Wake County Board of Education from 1993-1996. She has served on the Board of Education for eight years and presently is program chairman. Her constituents re-elected her to a second term in 1993.

In 1993, Mrs. Hoffman launched her vision for character education in Wake County. She continues to work in the community building support and consensus around character education and consults with other school systems and community organizations across the country. She frequently speaks to PTA's, civic organizations and church groups, and has presented at PREP, North Carolina Partners in Education, National School Board Association and North Carolina 4-H conferences.

Anne R. Lee

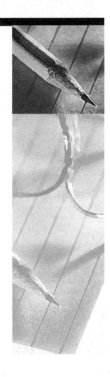

In December of 1993, Anne R. Lee was named to chair the Character Education Task Force for the Wake County School System in Raleigh, North Carolina. This 32-member group included parents, community representatives, principals, teachers, and students and was charged with designing Wake County's character education program.

Mrs. Lee is a former elementary school teacher, having taught in the Wake, Winston-Salem/Forsyth, and Charlotte/Mecklenburg systems in North Carolina. She is also a former assistant principal and counselor.

Being the mother of four children, Mrs. Lee has long been active as a school volunteer. She also is an instructor for parenting classes, covering such topics as discipline, communication, family relationships, and developing good character and healthy self-esteem. She has been a frequent guest speaker for civic clubs, church groups, women's conferences, PTA's and school faculties on such issues as character education, effective parenting, and classroom discipline.

Mrs. Lee received a Bachelor of Arts in Education from Duke University and a Master of Education from the University of North Carolina at Chapel Hill. She presently oversees the character education program for Wake County, chairs the Community Involvement Committee, consults with other school systems, and serves on the steering committee for the Partnership in Character Education which administers a $750,000 federally-funded grant for the state of North Carolina. She has presented at numerous character education conferences including the PREP, CEP, Communities in Schools, NCASCD, NC School Boards Association, Character Counts!, and the State of South Carolina conferences.

REFERENCES

RESOURCE PUBLICATIONS

Bennett, W.J., ed. (1993). *The Book of Virtues: A Treasury of Great Moral Stories.* New York: Simon & Schuster.

Bennett, W.J., ed. (1996). *The Book of Virtues for Young People.* N.J.: Silver Burdett.

Benson, P.L., J. Galbraith and P. Espeland (1995). *What Kids Need to Succeed.* Minneapolis: Free Spirit Publishing.

Coles, R. (1989). *The Call of Stories: Teaching and the Moral Imagination.* Boston: Houghton Mifflin.

Huffman, H.A. (1994). *Developing a Character Education Program.* Alexandria, Va.: Association for Supervision and Curriculum Development.

Kidder, R.M. (1995). *How Good People Make Tough Choices.* New York: William Morrow.

Kilpatrick, W. (1994). *Books That Build Character.* New York: Simon & Schuster.

Kilpatrick, W. (1992). *Why Johnny Can't Tell Right From Wrong.* New York: Simon & Schuster.

Lickona, J. (1991). *Educating for Character: How Our Schools Can Teach Respect and Responsibility.* New York: Bantam Books.

Vincent, P. (1995) *Developing Character in Students.* Chapel Hill, N.C.: New View.

Vincent, P. (1996) *Promising Practices in Character Education.* Chapel Hill, N.C.: Character Development Group

Wynne, E.A. and K. Ryan (1992). *Reclaiming Our Schools: A Handbook on Teaching Character, Academics, and Discipline.* New York: Merrill.

RESOURCE ORGANIZATIONS

Center for the Advancement of Ethics and Character. Boston University, School of Education, 605 Commonwealth Ave, Boston, MA 02215; Phone (617) 353-3262; Dr. Kevin Ryan, Director.

Center for the Fourth and Fifth Rs (Respect and Responsibility). Education Department, SUNY Cortland, Cortland, NY 13045; Phone (607) 753-7881; Dr. Thomas Lickona, Director, (607) 753-2455.

The Character Counts Coalition. 4640 Admiralty Way, Suite 1001, Marina del Rey, CA 90292; Phone (310) 306-1868. (See Josephson Institute)

The Character Education Partnership. 1250 North Pitt Street, Alexandria, VA 22314; Phone (703) 739-9515; Fax (703) 739-4967.

Character Development Group. P.O. Box 9211, Chapel Hill, NC 27515-9211; Phone (919) 967-2110; Fax (919) 967-2139.

The Child Development Project. Developmental Studies Center, 2000 Embarcadero, Suite 305, Oakland, CA 94606-5300; Phone (510) 533-0213.

The Joseph and Edna Josephson Institute of Ethics. Josephson Institute, 4640 Admiralty Way, Suite 1001, Marina del Rey, CA 90292; Phone (310) 306-1868; Fax (310) 827-1864. (See Character Counts Coalition).

Personal Responsibility Education Program (PREP). The Network for Educational Development, 13157 Olive Spur Road, St. Louis, MO 63141; Phone (314) 576-3535, ext. 130; FAX (314) 576-4996.

The Jefferson Center for Character Education. 202 South Lake Ave., #240, Pasadena, CA 91101; Phone (818) 792-8130.

Appendices:
Character
Education
Materials

WAKE COUNTY PUBLIC SCHOOL SYSTEM

CHARACTER EDUCATION SURVEY

In recent years a consensus has emerged among educators, parents, and community members on the need to address the negative influences that are eroding our society. Increases in violence, disrespect, poverty, illiteracy, sexual promiscuity, drug abuse, and the breakdown of the family serve as reminders every day that we have serious societal problems that must be addressed through the collaborative efforts of our community.

Wake County
Character Education
Survey, Page 1

In November of 1993, Judy Hoffman, chairman of the Wake County Board of Education, focused attention on this concern by requesting that the Wake County Board of Education establish a Character Education Task Force. Board members unanimously endorsed this initiative and a thirty-two member task force, composed of parents, teachers, students, administrators, and community representatives, was named. Task force members were asked to develop a list of core character traits which could serve as the basis for a formal character education program. The objective of this program would be to affirm and support positive character development in our children, in concert with the goals of parents, through the active involvement of school personnel and the community.

Over the last several months, members of the Character Education Task Force have identified and described eight core character traits on which to focus. The list of traits is not intended to be exhaustive; however, it represents consensus among a diverse group of people who were chosen to represent our entire community.

This survey has been designed to elicit input on the recommended traits from parents, teachers, students, and other members of the community to determine if these are the areas which should be the basis for the development of a system-wide character education program.

The task force members would appreciate your completing this survey and returning it to the most convenient school within one week of receipt. Thank you for your participation in this very important endeavor!

(OVER)

3600 Wake Forest Road ■ P.O. Box 28041 ■ Raleigh, North Carolina 27611 ■ Telephone: (919) 850-1766

CHARACTER EDUCATION SURVEY

Complete using a #2 pencil. Please do not fold or bend.

Please fill in the bubble beside the word or phrase that best describes you:
- ☐ Parent
- ☐ Student
- ☐ Community Member
- ☐ Teacher/Media Specialist/Counselor
- ☐ Administrator
- ☐ Other Staff Member

PLEASE READ THE CHARACTER TRAITS AND DEFINITIONS BELOW, THEN FILL IN THE BUBBLE AFTER EACH CHARACTER TRAIT THAT YOU BELIEVE SHOULD BE INCLUDED IN THE CHARACTER EDUCATION PROGRAM.

COURAGE
Having the determination to do the right thing even when others don't; the strength to follow your conscience rather than the crowd. Attempting difficult things that are worthwhile. ☐

GOOD JUDGMENT
Choosing worthy goals and setting proper priorities. Thinking through the consequences of your actions. Basing decisions on practical wisdom and good sense. ☐

INTEGRITY
Having the inner strength to be truthful, trustworthy, and honest in all things.
Acting justly and honorably. ☐

KINDNESS
Being considerate, courteous, helpful, and understanding of others. Showing care, compassion, friendship, and generosity. Treating others as you would like to be treated. ☐

Wake County
Character Education
Survey, Page 2

PERSEVERANCE
Being persistent in pursuit of worthy objectives in spite of difficulty, opposition, or discouragement. Exhibiting patience and having the fortitude to try again when confronted with delays, mistakes, or failures. ☐

RESPECT
Showing high regard for authority, for other people, for self, for property, and for country. Understanding that all people have value as human beings. ☐

RESPONSIBILITY
Being dependable in carrying out obligations and duties. Showing reliability and consistency in words and conduct. Being accountable for your own actions. Being committed to active involvement in your community. ☐

SELF-DISCIPLINE
Demonstrating hard work and commitment to purpose. Regulating yourself for improvement and restraining from inappropriate behaviors. Being in proper control of your words, actions, impulses, and desires. Choosing abstinence from premarital sex, drugs, alcohol, tobacco, and other harmful substances and behaviors. Doing your best in all situations. ☐

IF YOU WOULD LIKE TO MAKE ANY COMMENTS, PLEASE PLACE ON A SEPARATE PIECE OF PAPER AND RETURN WITH YOUR CHARACTER EDUCATION SURVEY.

PLEASE RETURN WITHIN ONE WEEK TO THE MOST CONVENIENT SCHOOL.

Character Education Survey Final Results

TRAIT	N	MISSING N	% AGREEING
Respect	24474	3724	86.80%
Kindness	23964	4234	85.00%
Responsibility	23906	4292	84.80%
Courage	23718	4480	84.10%
Good Judgment	23523	4675	83.40%
Integrity	23349	4849	82.80%
Self Discipline	23270	4928	82.50%
Perseverance	21937	6261	77.80%

A total of 28,198 surveys were scanned.

There are approximately 1500 survey forms that are unscannable because they were photocopied or damaged.

Character Education Survey Responses

Written Survey Responses

Total Letters Received	Overall Supportive	Overall Critical	Undecided/ Not clear	Total
	413	178	77	668
Criticism/ Suggestions				
Should be taught at home	58	110	25	193
Suggestions for specific traits	129	13	5	147
Concerned about academics	17	42	10	69
Must be modeled, not taught	36	20	8	65
Survey is a waste of time/money	33	15	6	54
Who will teach, what will be taught	22	14	12	48
Religion is the answer	30	10	6	46
Traits are already being taught	23	13	4	40
More discipline is needed	20	5	8	33
Integrate into curriculum	23	13	4	40
Won't work	0	17	1	18
Only for those who need it	8	4	1	13
Butt out! It's my business!	0	9	0	9

Character Education Plan — Parallel Strands

Character Education Task Force	Schools	Central Office
• Initiate process to determine what character traits (common values) can be agreed on to be specifically supported and enhanced collaboratively by the school, home and community, e.g., honesty, respect, etc. • Compile input from each school community and central office staff to determine systemwide character traits list. • Establish how to support character traits through: - Curriculum and Instruction - Parent Programs (preschool through high school) - Community Efforts	• Share list of character traits with school staff, students, where appropriate, and parents. • Receive input to determine additions, deletions, priorities. • Provide input to character education task force. • Identify what teacher behaviors support character education traits (modeling). • Determine how existing school programs support character traits and where additional initiatives may be needed to ensure a caring environment that supports the success of each student.	• Share list of character traits with central office staff. • Receive input to determine additions, deletions, priorities. • Provide input to character education task force. • Identify areas in the curriculum which support/reinforce character traits. • Identify programs to support character traits. • Identify leadership and staff development programs to support character traits.

Character Education

The Wake County Character Education Task Force was formally organized on December 13, 1993, during a meeting at the Wake County Public School System administration building. The meeting represented the culmination of months of research and discussion on how education could counter influences leading to school violence, disrespect for authority, selfishness, dishonesty, and a lack of discipline.

Wake County Board of Education Chairman Judy Hoffman launched the initiative, with the approval and encouragement of the school board. Hoffman named Anne Lee of Raleigh as chairman of the task force. She also appointed 31 other members — parents, community representatives, principals, teachers, and students.

The task force conducted its first working session in January of 1994. During that meeting, task force members agreed that despite cultural differences within the community, there is common ground; therefore, it is possible to identify and define core character traits acceptable to the entire community. Character traits were defined as inner qualities of an individual that are exemplified in behaviors or that incline the will to choose right over wrong. Task force members identified a long list of admirable character traits and behaviors, grouping and refining the list for further consideration.

At its meeting in February, the task force reviewed its original list and reduced it to eight core character traits and then channeled its energy toward developing tentative definitions for those eight traits. The traits and their definitions appear on the right-hand side of this page.

In April 1994, the school system distributed a Character Education survey to all parents, administrators, teachers, and fourth-, seventh-, and tenth-grade students. Other interested community members could pick up a survey at any school. The survey questions asked respondents which character traits they believed should be a focus for character education.

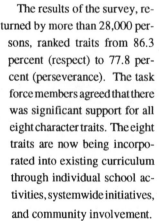

The results of the survey, returned by more than 28,000 persons, ranked traits from 86.3 percent (respect) to 77.8 percent (perseverance). The task force members agreed that there was significant support for all eight character traits. The eight traits are now being incorporated into existing curriculum through individual school activities, systemwide initiatives, and community involvement.

Character Education Brochure, September 1994

Character Traits

Courage —Having the determination to do the right thing even when others don't; the strength to follow your conscience rather than the crowd. Attempting difficult things that are worthwhile.

Good Judgment—Choosing worthy goals and setting proper priorities. Thinking through the consequences of your actions. Basing decisions on practical wisdom and good sense.

Integrity—Having the inner strength to be truthful, trustworthy, and honest in all things. Acting justly and honorably.

Kindness—Being considerate, courteous, helpful, and understanding of others. Showing care, compassion, friendship, and generosity. Treating others as you would like to be treated.

Perseverance—Being persistent in pursuit of worthy objectives in spite of difficulty, opposition, or discouragement. Exhibiting patience and having the fortitude to try again when confronted with delays, mistakes, or failures.

Respect—Showing high regard for authority, for other people, for self, for property, and for country. Understanding that all people have value as human beings.

Responsibility—Being dependable in carrying out obligations and duties. Showing reliability and consistency in words and conduct. Being accountable for your own actions. Being committed to active involvement in your community.

Self-discipline—Demonstrating hard work and commitment to purpose. Regulating yourself for improvement and restraining from inappropriate behaviors. Being in proper control of your words, actions, impulses, and desires. Choosing abstinence from premarital sex, drugs, alcohol, tobacco, and other harmful substances and behaviors. Doing your best in all situations.

WHAT ARE CHARACTER TRAITS?

◆ "Character traits" are inner qualities of an individual that are exemplified in behaviors or that incline the will to choose right over wrong.

◆ The character traits are a starting place for the "language of virtue and character" within public schools.

◆ The character traits on the front page are pivotal qualities of individual character broadly accepted in our community. These eight qualities form the basis of an effort to promote and inspire the development of good character in all students.

WHAT IS CHARACTER EDUCATION?

◆ Character education is learning about character traits and how they are linked to good behavior.

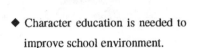
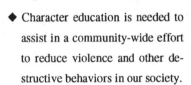

◆ It is learning how to make good decisions.

◆ It is learning that an individual can be in control of choices concerning his/her own behavior, and that such control is worthy of praise and respect.

◆ In Wake County schools, character education is not a separate course, nor is it an additional curriculum. Rather, it is a way of adapting existing educational materials to promote understanding and inspire development of good character traits among all students in every part of their school learning experiences.

WHY IMPLEMENT CHARACTER EDUCATION?

◆ Character education is needed to complement the efforts of parents, families, religious and civic organizations, and businesses in developing those qualities which ensure the continuity of a free and democratic society.

◆ Character education is needed to promote ethical behavior.

◆ Character education is needed to improve school environment.

◆ Character education is needed to assist in a community-wide effort to reduce violence and other destructive behaviors in our society.

◆ It is the right and responsible thing to do.

HOW WILL THE CHARACTER TRAITS BE TAUGHT?

◆ Character education will be integrated into the existing content areas, becoming a part of the general framework in which all education takes place. School personnel will make character part of the learning emphasis at all levels in every course and activity area.

◆ Character education will focus on the positive as much as possible. Negative qualities will be addressed only to the degree necessary to explain and affirm good character.

◆ Character education will treat topics seriously, but will do so in a manner that conveys a spirit of joyful enthusiasm.

♦ Character education efforts will vary depending on the age of the student. For example, discussions about the meaning of self-discipline will not address the issue of sexual abstinence except when, and at a level of sophistication, appropriate to a child's age.

♦ Teachers, while free to acknowledge their own views concerning the source of moral authority, will not promote their personal convictions. Philosophical or historical discussions at the secondary level may include various positions.

WHAT IS THE ROLE OF PARENTS?

♦ Parents have the primary responsibility for their child's education in moral character.

♦ While teachers have a legitimate role to play in promoting good character, they should never preempt the parents' primary responsibility in this area.

♦ School efforts to promote understanding and development of good character should reinforce and support the efforts of parents to model and teach good character at home. Teachers will never intentionally subvert or replace character goals that parents set for their children.

♦ Character education efforts in Wake County schools will remain limited to areas broadly supported by parents of school-aged children living in the community.

WHAT IS THE ROLE OF ADMINISTRATORS, TEACHERS, AND STAFF?

♦ School personnel will model good character in their attitudes and behaviors.

♦ School personnel will promote understanding and development of good character in all aspects of school life — on the playground, on the playing field, on the bus, in the cafeteria, and during extracurricular activities, as well as in the classroom.

♦ School personnel will promote a positive school environment in which good character can flourish.

HOW ABOUT THE ISSUE OF RELIGION?

♦ The source of moral authority is considered to be a matter of religious perspective. Character education will respect but will not promote a particular view regarding the source of moral authority.

♦ Character education will not be taught in a manner that is unique to a particular tradition regarding the nature of morality or the source of moral authority. The advocacy of particular views concerning these issues will be left to parents and to institutions concerned with religious education.

OBJECTIVES OF CHARACTER EDUCATION IN WAKE COUNTY SCHOOLS:

➤ To affirm and support the character goals of families who send their children to Wake County public schools by providing instruction on broadly supported traits of good character and affirming their practice.

➤ To develop an atmosphere in our public schools which considers good character something worthy of praise.

➤ To help children attending Wake County public schools learn to think before they act, to understand fundamental differences between right and wrong, and to make good decisions.

➤ To help children attending Wake County public schools to understand better what their community expects of them in terms of good character.

➤ To put the Wake County Public School System in a leadership position demonstrating to others how broadly based principles of good character can be taught in the public school setting.

WAKE
COUNTY
PUBLIC
SCHOOL
SYSTEM

September 1994

Nash-Rocky
Mount, NC,
Schools,
Character
Education
Brochure

CHARACTER EDUCATION

Nash-Rocky Mount Schools

Dr. Travis Twiford
SUPERINTENDENT

*Education worthy of its name is
essentially education of character.*
MARTIN BUBER

*To educate a person in mind and not morals
is to create a menace to society.*
THEODORE ROOSEVELT

*As Aristotle taught, people do not naturally
or spontaneously grow up to be morally excellent
or practically wise. They become so, if at all,
only as the result of a lifelong personal
and community effort.*
JON MOLINE

FINAL DRAFT

IDEAS FOR THE COMMUNITY

- Promote character in community sports programs.

- Conduct media promotions that promote character education.

- Hold seminars for employees that discuss ethics and character.

- Dedicate a religious service each month to a Character Concept.

- Coordinate community service activities.

- Partner with schools and provide on-site opportunities for students to observe teamwork and respect.

- Provide opportunities for parent education programs.

- Develop public service announcements and share them with local media.

- Model the concepts of respect, responsibility, integrity, caring, self-discipline, trustworthiness, fairness, and citizenship.

TASK FORCE MEMBERS

Jean Almand	H.H. Grier	Julie Love
Katherine Bagley	Phyllis Griffin	Jan Mills
Tonya Blalock	Denise Helms	Claudia Moore
Lela Chesson	Marsh Holloman	Tekiya Mozell
Charles Davis	Monta Hunter	Adam Murray
Lari Dirkmaat	Bob Hyatt	Elizabeth Ohree
Wayne Doll	Margaret Hyman	Charles Robinson
Brenda Edge	Franklin Lamm	Bryan Sexton
John Gibson	Gaylord Lehman	Gail Stafford
		Edythe Tweedy

SCHOOL BOARD MEMBERS

Jan Mills–Chairperson	Frances Harrison
Chalmers Nunn–Vice Chair	Richard Horner
Jean Almand	Ernie Murray
John T. Avent	Nehemiah Smith
David Brown	Edythe Tweedy
Joseph Gurganus	

CHARACTER TRAITS AND DEFINITIONS

Trustworthiness: Having an inner strength of integrity, honesty, and loyalty in order to be worthy of the confidence of others.

Respect: Showing a high regard for authority, for others, and for self through courtesy and cooperation, and through freedom from racism and all other forms of prejudice and bigotry.

Responsibility: Demonstrating accountability for one's own words and actions and displaying dependability in carrying out one's obligations and duties.

Caring: Showing understanding of others by treating them with kindness, compassion, generosity, and a forgiving spirit.

Fairness: Promoting justice and fairness in dealing with others and recognizing the uniqueness and value of each individual.

Citizenship: Demonstrating a commitment to community and country through law-abiding behavior and community service.

Perseverance: Pursuing worthy objectives with great persistence, determination, and patience, and exhibiting fortitude when confronted with adversity or failure.

Courage: Doing the right thing in the face of difficulty and risking unpopularity while holding fast to one's ethical standards.

Self-Discipline: Controlling one's words, actions, and desires; renouncing violence; and choosing abstinence from premarital sex, drugs, alcohol, tobacco, and other destructive behaviors.

PROGRAM FOUNDATION

The Nash-Rocky Mount Character Education Task Force was formally organized on December 12, 1995 during a meeting at Nash Central Junior High School. The meeting represented a request by the Nash-Rocky Mount School Board to pursue community input for the initiation of a program to focus on character development of students.

During the initial meeting, the Task Force agreed that common ground exists within a community of diverse cultures. The Task Force was charged to identify character traits important and acceptable to the community. Character traits are defined as inner qualities of an individual exemplified in behaviors or that incline the will to choose right over wrong. After several meetings, the Task Force identified nine character traits as foundations for character development in students.

During a later meeting, the Task Force defined each of the nine traits to enhance the school and community efforts to teach character. These efforts are to reinforce the traditional values and positive character traits that originate in the home.

Join with us as we unite to model and teach character to our young people. We all share the responsibility to develop a community of character.

Lari Dirkmaat
Chairperson

Good character must start at home, must be taught, must be modeled, must be a united community effort and will lead to success.
ANONYMOUS

ELEVEN PRINCIPLES of Effective Character Education

By Tom Lickona Eric Schaps Catherine Lewis

Character Education Partnership

There is no single script for effective character education, but there are some important basic principles. The following eleven principles serve as criteria that schools and other groups can use to plan a character education effort and to evaluate available character education programs, books, and curriculum resources.

1. Character education promotes core ethical values as the basis of good character. Character education holds, as a starting philosophical principle, that there are widely shared, pivotally important core ethical values — such as caring, honesty, fairness, responsibility, and respect for self and others — that form the basis of good character. A school committed to character education explicitly names and publicly stands for these values; promulgates them to all members of the school community; defines them in terms of behaviors that can be observed in the life of the school; models these values; studies and discusses them; uses them as the basis of human relations in the school; celebrates their manifestations in the school and community; and upholds them by making all school members accountable to standards of conduct consistent with the core values.

In a school committed to developing character, these core values are treated as a matter of obligation, as having a claim on the conscience of the individual and community. Character education asserts that the validity of these values, and our obligation to uphold them, derive from the fact that such values affirm our human dignity; they promote the development and welfare of the individual person; they serve the common good; they meet the classical ethical tests of reversibility (Would you want to be treated this way?) and universalizability (Would you want all persons to act this way in a similar situation?); and they define our rights and responsibilities in a democratic society. The school makes clear that these basic human values transcend religious and cultural differences and express our common humanity.

2. "Character" must be comprehensively defined to include thinking, feeling, and behavior. In an effective character education program, character is broadly conceived to encompass the cognitive, emotional, and behavioral aspects of the moral life. Good character consists of understanding, caring about, and acting upon core ethical values. The task of character education therefore is to help students and all other members of the learning community know "the good," value it, and act upon it. As people grow in their character, they will develop an increasingly refined understanding of the core values, a deeper commitment to living according to those values, and a stronger tendency to behave in accordance with those values.

3. Effective character education requires an intentional, proactive, and comprehensive approach that promotes the core values in all phases of school life. Schools committed to character education look at themselves through a moral lens and see how virtually everything that goes on in school affects the values and character of students. An intentional and proactive approach plans deliberate ways to develop character, rather than simply waiting for opportunities to occur. A comprehensive approach uses all aspects of schooling — the teacher's example, the discipline policy, the academic curriculum (including the drug, alcohol, and sex education curriculum), the

instructional process, the assessment of learning, the management of the school environment, relationships with parents, and so on — as opportunities for character development. "Stand alone" character education programs can be useful first steps or helpful elements of an ongoing effort but must not be considered a substitute for a holistic approach that integrates character development into every aspect of school life.

4. The school must be a caring community. The school itself must embody good character. It must progress toward becoming a microcosm of the civil, caring, and just society we seek to create as a nation. The school can do this by becoming a moral community that helps students form caring attachments to adults and to each other. These caring relationships will foster both the desire to learn and the desire to be a good person. All children and adolescents have a need to belong, and they are more likely to internalize the values and expectations of groups that meet this need. The daily life of classrooms, as well as all other parts of the school environment (e.g., the corridors, cafeteria, playground, and school bus), must be imbued with core values such as concern and respect for others, responsibility, kindness, and fairness.

5. To develop character, students need opportunities for moral action. In the ethical as in the intellectual domain, students are constructive learners; they learn best by doing. To develop good character, they need many and varied opportunities to apply values such as responsibility and fairness in everyday interactions and discussions. By grappling with real-life challenges — how to divide the labor in a cooperative learning group, how to reach consensus in a class meeting, how to

carry out a service learning project, how to reduce fights on the playground -students develop practical understanding of the requirements of fairness, cooperation, and respect. Through repeated moral experiences, students can also develop and practice the moral skills and behavioral habits that make up the action side of character.

6. Effective character education includes a meaningful and challenging academic curriculum that respects all learners and helps them succeed. Character education and academic learning must not be conceived as separate spheres; rather there must be a strong, mutually supportive relationship. In a caring classroom and school where students feel liked and respected by their teachers and fellow students, students are more likely to work hard and achieve. Reciprocally, when students are enabled to succeed at the work of school, they are more likely to feel valued and cared about as persons. Because students come to school with diverse skills, interests and needs, a curriculum that helps all students succeed will be one whose content and pedagogy are sophisticated enough to engage all learners. That means moving beyond a skill-and-drill, paper-and-pencil curriculum to one that is inherently interesting and meaningful for students. A character education school makes effective use of active teaching and learning methods such as cooperative learning, problem-solving approaches, experience-based projects, and the like. One of the most authentic ways to respect children is to respect the way they learn.

7. Character education should strive to develop students' intrinsic motivation. As students develop good character, they develop a stronger inner commitment to doing what

their moral judgment tells them is right. Schools, especially in their approach to discipline, should strive to develop this intrinsic commitment to core values. They should minimize reliance on extrinsic rewards and punishments that distract students' attention from the real reasons to behave responsibly: the rights and needs of self and others. Responses to rule-breaking should give students opportunities for restitution and foster the students' understanding of the rules and willingness to abide by them in the future. Similarly, within the academic curriculum, intrinsic motivation should be fostered in every way possible. This can be done by helping students experience the challenge and interest of subject matter, the desire to work collaboratively with other students, and the fulfillment of making a positive difference in another person's life or in their school or community.

8. The school staff must become a learning and moral community in which all share responsibility for character education and attempt to adhere to the same core values that guide the education of students. Three things need attention here. First, all school staff — teachers, administrators, counselors, coaches, secretaries, cafeteria workers, playground aides, bus drivers — must be involved in learning about, discussing, and taking ownership of the character education effort. All of these adults must model the core values in their own behavior and take advantage of the other opportunities they have to influence the character of the students with whom they come into contact. Second, the same values and norms that govern the life of students must govern the collective life of the adult members of the school community. If students are to be treated as constructive learners, so must

adults. They must have extended staff development and many opportunities to observe and then try out ways of integrating character education practices into their work with students. If students are given opportunities to work collaboratively and participate in decision making that improves classrooms and school, so must adults. If a school's staff members do not experience mutual respect, fairness, and cooperation in their adult relationships, they are less likely to be committed to teaching those values to students. Third, the school must find and protect time for staff reflection on moral matters. School staff, through faculty meetings and smaller support groups, should be regularly asking: What positive, character-building experiences is the school already providing for its students? What negative moral experiences (e.g., peer cruelty, student cheating, adult disrespect of students, littering of the grounds) is the school currently failing to address? And what important moral experiences (e.g., cooperative learning, school and community service, opportunities to learn about and interact with people from different racial, ethnic, and socioeconomic backgrounds) is the school now omitting? What school practices are at odds with its professed core values and desire to develop a caring school community? Reflection of this nature is an indispensable condition for developing the moral life of a school.

9. Character education requires moral leadership from both staff and students. For character education to meet the criteria outlined thus far, there must be leaders (a principal, another administrator, a lead teacher) who champions the effort and, at least initially, a character education committee (or several such support groups, each focused on a particular aspect of the character effort) with responsibility for long-range planning and program implementation. Over time, the functions of this committee may be taken on by the school's regular governing bodies. Students should also be brought into roles of moral leadership through student government, peer conflict mediation programs, cross-age tutoring, and the like.

10. The school must recruit parents and community members as full partners in the character-building effort. A school's character education mission statement should state explicitly what is true: Parents are the first and most important moral educators of their children. Next, the school should take pains at every stage to communicate with parents about the school's goals and activities regarding character development — and how families can help. To build trust between home and school, parents should be represented on the character leadership committee that does the planning, the school should actively reach out to "disconnected" subgroups of parents, and all parents need to be informed about — and have a chance to react and consent to — the school's proposed core values and how the school proposes to try to teach them. Finally, schools and families will enhance the effectiveness of their partnership if they recruit the help of the wider community — businesses, religious institutions, youth organizations, the government, and the media — in promoting the core ethical values.

1 l. Evaluation of character education should assess the character of the school, the school staff's functioning as character educators, and the extent to which students manifest good character. Effective character education must include an effort to assess progress. Three broad kinds of outcomes merit attention:

(a) The character of the school: To what extent is the school becoming a more caring community? This can be assessed, for example, with surveys that ask students to indicate the extent to which they agree with statements such as, "Students in this school [classroom] respect and care about each other," and "This school [classroom] is like a family."

(b) The school staffs growth as character educators: To what extent have adult staff — teaching faculty, administrators, and support personnel — developed understandings of what they can do to foster character development? Personal commitment to doing so? Skills to carry it out? Consistent habits of acting upon their developing capacities as character educators?

(c) Student character: To what extent do students manifest understanding of, commitment to, and action upon the core ethical values? Schools can, for example, gather data on various character related behaviors: Has student attendance gone up? Fights and suspensions gone down? Vandalism declined? Drug incidents diminished?

Schools can also assess the three domains of character (knowing feeling, and behaving) through anonymous questionnaires that measure student moral judgment (for example, "Is cheating on a test wrong?"), moral commitment ("Would you cheat if you were sure you wouldn't get caught?") and self reported moral behavior ("How many times have you cheated on a test or major assignment in the past year?"). Such questionnaires can be administered at the beginning of a school's character initiative to get a baseline and again at later points to assess progress.

For More Information Contact: The Character Education Partnership 1-800-988-8081

Sample Character Education Staff Awareness Session(s)

- Divide the staff in groups of 8 or 16, depending on staff size. Have chart paper, markers, and masking tape for each group.
- Give overview of character education.
- Assign each group one of the character traits and have them select a recorder.
- Have each group:
  - Read the definition of their trait
  - Brainstorm and record specific examples of how adults in this school model this trait to other adults and students.
  - Using another sheet of chart paper, brainstorm and then record specific examples of how the total school program has been reflective of exemplifying this trait.
  - Using a third sheet of chart paper, brainstorm and then list practices or barriers in place that counteract this character trait.
  - Using a fourth sheet of chart paper, brainstorm and then record two schoolwide practices or activities which could be implemented to exemplify or reinforce this character trait.
  - Have each group post their charts. Give 5 minutes for each group to present their ideas.
- Collect all charts and have someone summarize this information so it can be distributed back to all staff members.
- Ask teachers to conduct this same activity with students. In elementary schools this may mean assigning one trait per grades K-3 and two traits to grades 4 and 5. In middle and high schools, this may mean assigning language arts and English class teachers this responsibility. Student responses should be summarized, distributed, and discussed by all staff members.

These sessions could give a foundation for starting to configure plans for incorporating character education into school activities and the curricula.

- Additional questions which might be used to examine character education:
  - How will we involve parents in character education?
  - How will we involve students?
  - How will we involve all staffmembers?
  - Where are character education traits exemplified in curriculum areas, such as literature, therefore, providing links for discussions and activities?

ADDITIONAL QUESTIONS FOR STAFF DEVELOPMENT

Curriculum

- Where in the curriculum does character education already exist?
- Where in the curriculum can we integrate character education?
- How can we present character traits not just as abstract concepts but in a concrete, meaningful way?
- How can we give our students visual concrete examples of what it means to be a person of character?
- Are we providing opportunities for our students to experience practicing good character through service opportunities, peer tutoring, cooperative learning, etc.?
- Do we utilize those "teachable moments" when we can apply the language of character to real life situations?

According to Dr. Thomas Lickona, character education involves three aspects:

1. Knowing the good. (head)
2. Desiring the good. (heart)
3. Doing the good. (hands)

- What teaching methods or curriculum ideas can we utilize to encourage these three elements?

Climate

- What aspects of our school climate are supportive of the practice of good character?

Wake County Public School System

- What current practices are detrimental to the development of good character?
- How are we emphasizing high expectations for student behavior?
- Does our behavior code/discipline policy reflect and encourage the desired character traits (e.g. responsibility, integrity, etc.)?
- Is our behavior code enforced consistently—day by day, class by class, and student by student?
- Do we support and encourage desirable behavior throughout the campus or only in our classroom?
- Do we feel it's not our problem or responsibility?
- Are there portions of the code we don't support or that need to be revised or eliminated?
- Are we ignoring enforcement of a rule even though we support it?
- What consequences do students experience when they break a rule? Are they fair? Are they consistent?
- Do we positively reinforce good character or just take it for granted?
- In what specific ways do we affirm good character?
- Do we model those traits we want to see in our students?

  Examples:

  - Do we treat our students respectfully, as well as demand respect from them?
  - Are we responsible about class preparation and returning papers promptly, as well as expecting responsible behavior from them?

- Is our school a positive place to be? Would you want to attend school here?
- What can we do to promote school pride and loyalty?

  In a large school it is extremely important for students to feel that they matter, that they are an important part of the community and that they have avenues to express their opinions and concerns. What would our students say about their significance as individuals?

- What procedures do we have in place for student input?
- How can a student express concerns or suggestions to teachers and administrators?
- Do classroom teachers get student input on classroom decisions, rules and procedures? What organizational ideas do we have to break down our large student body into smaller communities?
- Is our student council really functioning effectively or is it student government in name only?
- Does the average student know what the student council is doing and feel part of the democratic process?
- How could student government be involved in character education?
- In what other meaningful ways can students be involved?

Community

- What programs or practices already promote involvement with our larger community? Would some of those lend themselves to positively impacting character development?
- How can we involve others in the process of educating for character? of modeling good character?
- How can we involve all school personnel? (cafeteria workers, bus drivers, office staff, etc.)
- How can we involve the home?
- How can we involve the business community?
- How can we involve the faith community?
- How can we effectively tie character education into a community service component?
- How can we encourage broad use of the "language of character" throughout our community?

Ideas for Integrating Character Education

Memo to
Wake County
Principals

- Encourage teachers to begin each day, or a particular secondary class period, with a five-minute focus on character. Ideas might come from a newspaper article, a short passage from a book, a quotation, or a specific school or societal problem and how it might be alleviated.
- Have a poster contest on "Responsibility is..." or "Respect is ...," etc. Display posters.
- Ask students to write about a specific time when they, or someone they know, were faced with a tough decision and chose to be a person of character.
- Ask classes to research quotations from famous people on character in general, as well as the eight character traits. Display quotations.
- Have a media center scavenger hunt in which students utilize research skills in order to find such things as:
  - a quotation from Winston Churchill that defines perseverance
  - the U. S. president who established the Peace Corps
  - a book in which a character named Peg Leg Joe displayed respect and kindness.
- Have a "Rap for Character" or "Poetry for Character" day. Have students write raps or poems and share with classmates.
- Ask drama classes to develop short skits or pantomimes on matters of character. Present these to younger classes, followed by a discussion focusing on the application of the eight traits in making decisions.
- Use Paideia seminars to discuss issues of ethics and character
- Ask students to bring in current events which show either problems arising from a lack of character or positive benefits resulting from good character.
- Make a mural depicting situations where good character is being displayed.
- Try playing a simple game in physical education without establishing any rules. When things begin going awry, stop and discuss why games have rules, why we enjoy playing with others who follow the rules, etc.
- Brainstorm the qualities that make a hero or heroine (in literature, history, etc.). Extend the discussion to what character traits we admire in friends, teachers, etc. and why. Discuss whether many of our modern day "heroes" measure up to those standards.
- In studying a historical event, such as the holocaust or the American Revolution, discuss how the course of history might have been altered if individuals either had or had not displayed strong character.
- In physical education, or after school sports programs, discuss how character is important, e.g., the importance of self-discipline in training, the responsibility each person has to teammates, etc.
- Use short stories, historical events, quotes, dilemmas in fiction, etc., from curriculum as a springboard for discussion about character.
- Include character traits information in newsletters to parents.
- Ask a group (student council, Beta Club, school newspaper staff) to write some common school-related situations which require students to make a decision related to character. Conduct a survey to see what students would do in these situations. Publish the results in the school newspaper with comments and analysis of how student decisions match

the eight character traits.

- Ask the student council to be actively involved in planning character education activities.
- Encourage the PTA to sponsor character-related activities.
- Display students' art work or writing assignments focusing on character
- Study a famous person, highlighting the character traits which made this person famous.
- Create a list of "Eight Ways To Have a Great Day" using the eight character traits.
- Create a character education resource area in the media center.
- Create student committees to focus on high-priority, schoolwide issues or problems, such as:
    - improving cafeteria atmosphere
    - fostering good sportsmanship on playground or at athletic events
    - creating community service projects or community involvement projects
- Post sayings that encourage good character.
- Read and discuss biographies of accomplished individuals.
- Begin an exchange network or bulletin board by which teachers and administrators can share ways to promote character education.
- Design logos symbolizing each character trait.
- Analyze whether rules and expectations are stated positively and reinforce character traits.
- Make "big books" in grades K-2, which are compilations of the work of small groups of students writing and illustrating what they can do to encourage everyone to use the eight character traits.
- Have older students write their own books on one of the eight character traits and share with younger students.
- Make connections between conflict resolution and peer mediation programs and character traits.

Character Education: 25 Suggestions for Parents

The development of good character in children requires the efforts of both home and school, as well as those of community resources, such as religious and civic organizations. In an age when youth are increasingly influenced by the media and their peers, it is critically important that parents take an especially strong role in their children's moral development. The following recommendations are offered as food for thought.

1. Be authentic. Model good character in the home. Parents who refuse to cheat on income tax returns or take unfair advantage of their neighbors will have greater credibility when they discuss responsible citizenship or fairness with their children. Hold yourself and other family members accountable to high standards of good character.

2. Make clear statements about your values and beliefs to your children. Let them know where you stand on important issues. Be sure they understand the principles or the "why" behind your beliefs.

3. Show respect for your spouse, your children, and other family members. Teach your children to treat elders with courtesy and respect, to practice sensitivity and empathy.

4. Model and teach your children good manners and insist that all family members use good manners (please, thank you, etc.).

5. Demonstrate and encourage healthy ways to resolve conflict both inside and outside your home.

6. Have family meals together (without television) as often as possible. Even if the meal is a take-out order of fast food, try to sit down as a family to eat it. Use this as an opportunity to talk with your children and to listen to their concerns.

7. Plan as many family activities as possible. Be sure to involve your children in the planning. Let them know that you value their recommendations. Have fun together!

8. Do not provide access to drugs or alcohol for your children. Model appropriate behavior regarding alcohol and drugs.

9. Worship together as a family. Recent studies verify that youth who have strong religious convictions are less likely to drop out of school or engage in delinquent behavior.

10. Plan family service projects or civic activities. Sample projects include volunteering at a shelter or soup kitchen, mowing the lawn for an elderly neighbor, taking a meal to a new neighbor, or working together on an environmental concern.

11. Read to your children and keep good literature in the home. Much literature contains a rich source of material for character development.

12. Limit your children's spending money. Help them to develop an appreciation for non-material rewards. Provide opportunities for them to work and to earn those things they desire.

13. Discuss the holidays and their history. Use these opportunities to help your children appreciate the great figures in history and their contributions to our lives. Have family celebrations and establish family traditions.

14. Share your heroes with your children. Explain why you admire certain people and the specific character traits they possess.

15. Use situations that occur (an incident at school, a television news report, a movie, etc.) to spark family discussions on important

issues. Capitalize on the "teachable moment."

16. Allow your children to solve their own day-to-day problems. Discuss options and offer encouragement, but avoid "taking over" unless it is necessary.

17. Assign home responsibilities (taking out the trash, washing dishes, etc.) for all family members. Even very young children can be responsible for simple tasks. As children mature allow them to experience more and more opportunities to be responsible.

18. Set clear expectations for your children and consistently hold them accountable for their actions. Make sure that they know the rules and consequences. When they break the rules, be sure that they experience appropriate consequences.

19. Look for opportunities to reward wise decisions and desirable behavior, rather than focusing on the negative.

20. Provide positive activities (sports, hobbies, music lessons, service projects, scouts, etc.) and adequate supervision for your child. (Much of the substance abuse and inappropriate sexual behavior of adolescents occurs in homes when parents are away.)

21. Learn to say <u>no</u> and mean it. Despite the child's protests, a parent's most loving act is often to stand firm and prohibit the child's participation in a potentially hurtful activity.

22. Know where your children are, whom they are with, and what they are doing. At the risk of being accused of being "old-fashioned," insist on meeting their friends and their parents.

23. Refuse to cover for your children or make excuses for their inappropriate behavior. For example, if your child skips class, let him or her suffer the consequences. Lying for the child sends a very powerful message about the parents' values.

24. Pay attention to the television shows, videos, and movies that your children are watching. While there are some very fine materials available, there is also much harmful material easily accessible to our youth. If you learn that your child has viewed something that you find objectionable, candidly share your feelings and discuss why the material offends your values.

25. Remember that you are the adults! Children don't need another buddy, but they desperately need a parent who cares enough to set and enforce appropriate limits for their behavior. Often, being able to say, "My dad won't let me..." provides a convenient escape for a student who really didn't want to participate in a questionable activity.

The majority of these suggestions have been adapted by the Wake County Public School System from a list written by Dr. Helen LeGette at Burlington City Schools, Burlington, NC. Additional input was received from the Center for the Advancement of Ethics and Character, Boston University.

A Report from Pleasant Union Elementary School's Character Education Committee

The Character Education Committee at Pleasant Union Elementary School in Raleigh, N.C. was organized at the beginning of the 1994-95 school year by principal Susan Jordan. The committee consists of a teacher as chairperson, a teacher from each grade level, a teacher's assistant, the school guidance counselor, and a specialist teacher. The following year several parent volunteers were added to the committee. The 1996-97 committee was open to any parent interested in Character Education. The committee meets monthly as needed to discuss ongoing programs, new ideas and community projects.

One of the first tasks of the committee was to write a missions statement for our committee. Later a teacher survey was distributed to determine what was already being done in the school for character education and identify some needs/ideas our committee could use in planning and setting goals for the year.

Some of our project ideas include:

• A separate section in the library designated for character education books which can be checked out by teachers, students and parents. A character education bibliography is available to assist in locating specific books.

• Character Education material has been included in Pleasant Union's School Home Page on the Internet written by our media specialist.

• The teacher/parent resource shelf in the media center includes literature depicting the character traits, booklists and teaching ideas/materials for character education.

• Parents who volunteer in the classroom reading character-based stories and using activities/games to teach the character traits.

• Character Education Notebook where parents can record and share ideas/materials they have used in the classroom. Character traits highlighted on the school's own morning television news program.

• Visual aids such as posters, quotes and trait definitions throughout the school.

• National Character Counts Week observed with spots on morning news and guest readers in the classrooms.

• Community service projects annually by each classroom as a means of putting traits into action.

• Bulletin board in school foyer dedicated to character education and featuring artwork, essays, etc. done by students. This reminds visitors and students of the school's ongoing emphasis on character education.

• Contests and recognitions for student's character-based work.

• "Thanks Giving" board in school's foyer during Thanksgiving season provided space for students to thank those who had demonstrated character such as kindness to them. The board filled so quickly, a second one was needed.

• Pleasant Union's PTA Newsletter regularly features Character Education news and information for parents.

• "Read Aloud Week" that encourages and educates parents on selecting and reading character based stories to their children.

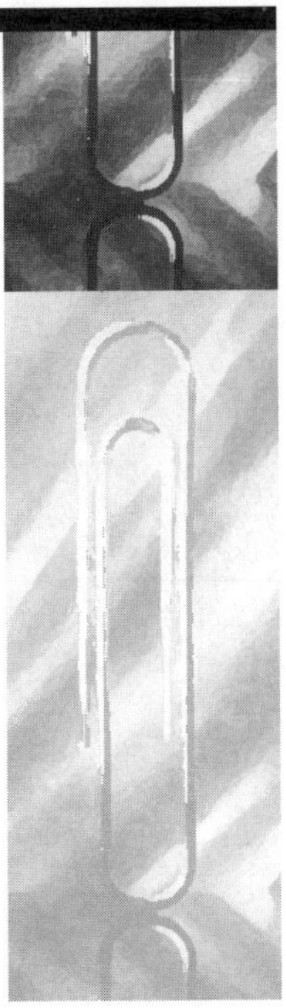

2812 Elsbeth Court
Wake Forest, North Carolina 27587
(919) 850-0366; (919) 556-0540

May 4, 1995

Mrs. Molly Carrier
Eighth Grade Language Arts
Wake Forest-Rolesville Middle School
1800 South Main Street
Wake Forest, North Carolina 27587

Dear Mrs. Carrier,

The Wake County Board of Education has really emphasized "character education" this year and I just want to thank you for all your wonderful efforts in that regard. I believe you have always taught good character values, even before the Board started promoting them. You actually live them.

I believe one primarily teaches character by example and your example has be a most exemplary one. You have treated your students with respect and consideration; and following your fine example, they in turn have treated you with the same consideration. Some other teachers have given "character education" assignments which are very inconsistent with their own behavior and attitudes toward their students and people in general; I believe those assignments have failed miserably. It's sort of like saying, "do as I say, not as I do." I have been unable to support superficial assignments of that nature from adults who lack good character qualities.

Brad's assignment from you last evening was to write a paper about a hero. He chose Robert E. Lee. You asked the students to name four traits they admire in their hero. Brad chose wonderful character traits and told how Robert E. Lee exemplified those qualities. I do not know how you will grade Brad's paper, but I think it's the best paper he has ever written. I was so pleased to learn about the character traits Brad admires and why. What a wonderful assignment!

Please know that I sincerely appreciate all your efforts on Brad's behalf this year. You are a wonderful credit to your profession and I feel so fortunate that Brad was the recipient of all your many lessons this year, lessons about language arts, fine character and life in general. Please know that you have our utmost respect and gratitude.

Sincerely,

Lynn Snow
cc: Ann Lee, Suzanne King, Judy Hoffman, Danny Barnes

Letter from
a parent

I've got character!

The Public Information Office needs your help in letting the media know about the good things done by great people associated with our schools. Each month, we'll send out a set of news releases advising the media about folks whose conduct exemplifies one of the eight key traits emphasized each month through character education. If you know about someone wonderful, we want to know about them, too. Use this form or anything like it to submit nominations to your school's character education representative, who will forward them to us.

School name and phone number: _____

Full name and title of nominee: _____

Full name and title of nominator: _____

The nominee knows he/she may be contacted by the media: _____ yes _____ no

I have parental permission of any student involved: _____ yes _____ no

I've given a copy of this nomination to my principal: _____ yes _____ no

Please print legibly or type nomination below. Include a positive anecdote that clearly explains why the nominee exemplifies a specific character trait.

This form may be copied and used to submit nominations each month for different character traits. Nominations for the February trait of Integrity are due by Tuesday, Jan. 28. Nominations may be sent by courier to Jill Warren Lucas in the Public Information Office, or faxed to 850-1618.

Character
Nomination Form,
The Exchange,
January 9, 1997,
Wake County
Public Schools

Sample News Releases to Local Papers

The following individuals have been selected as exemplary models of self-discipline, the Wake County Public Schools' focus character trait for January.

Reginald Vick, head custodian at Knightdale Elementary in Knightdale; nominated by the Knightdale Elementary staff:

"Reginald Vick always reports to work early and is among the last to leave. He gets here early to make sure we have warm, clean rooms. He walks the campus to make sure it is a safe place. And we always can count on him to be on hand if we need to stay late.

"The school children are very important to Mr. Vick, who has four children of his own and three foster children. He makes time to visit classrooms to read to students and often can be seen patiently working with children who need extra help. During black history month, our students agreed they would rather have him around than Michael Jordan.

"Also, Mr. Vick has proved himself a master at problem-solving. When the ice and bad weather created problems last year for carpool lines, he met Principal Pamela Peters at the school to take kindergarten classes on field trips, and to counsel those youngsters who need a father figure. Because of all this and more, we salute Mr. Vick as Knightdale Elementary's finest example of self-discipline."

Nolan Hayes, 12th-grade student at Fuquay-Varina High in Fuquay-Varina; nominated by Coach Bill Brown:

"Athlete Nolan Hayes is Fuquay-Varina High's definition of self-discipline. A glance at Nolan's activities explains why: Nolan is editor of the student newspaper, starting point guard (two years in a row) for the basketball team, No. 2 runner on the cross-country team (he's ranked fourth in the state), and a straight-A honor student whose list of AP classes and academic accomplishments is as long and varied as his list of friends.

"A master of time management, Nolan can prioritize, organize, and focus with the best. On top of it all, Nolan is a genuinely nice guy; teachers and students alike admire him and delight in his company. To do all that, you *have* to be disciplined. And to see Nolan do all that, we have to be impressed."

Action Ideas for the Community Involvement Committee

- Present the eight character traits to the Wake County Commissioners and ask them to join us to publicly adopt these traits for Wake County to increase awareness, to promote a uniform language, and to serve as leaders.
- Develop a speakers bureau; take presentations on character to all segments of our community.
- Replicate this conference model yearly and have miniconferences targeting specific segments of the community, e.g., businesses, civic organizations, places of worship, judicial system.
- Expand collaborations with businesses, schools, civic groups, places of worship.
- Encourage more media attention to character development and the importance of community involvement.
- Feature students and what they are doing in character education presentations and news releases.
- Create a package to give to civic organizations sharing ideas on how to promote character development.
- Encourage museums and public libraries to have programs and kits highlighting the traits, e.g., History Museum, Art, Natural Sciences, Life and Science, Exploris, Park System.
- Highlight this community as a community that values good character; keep it in the forefront, continue the momentum, widen the audience.
- Get businesses to buy into character training.

Suggestions resulting from Community Character Forum, Wake County, 1996

- Expand programs which provide mentors, tutors, role models, buddies.
- Develop cooperative relationships with other agencies that work with youth, recognizing common goals and developing a common language.

Action Ideas for the Business Community

- Adopt Wake County's eight character traits and display them in your business.
- Establish Community Service Awards recognizing citizenship, leadership, service, and exemplary character.
- Be proactive in teaching ethics and establishing expectations for ethical behavior in the business community and community at large.
- Set up the expectation that your business will be an organization of character.
- Provide training in ethics for your employees.
- Identify business leaders who can effectively share their personal "character story" - struggles and successes - with students and/or the media.
- Provide 1/2 day off a month for employees to go into schools to work with children (paid release time).
- Encourage and affirm the display of good character in your employees, especially youth.
- Highlight the importance of character in business ads, on billboards, commercials, etc.
- Utilize the language of character in business meetings and in communication with employees and customers.

Action Ideas for Civic Organizations

- Provide service opportunities for children, e.g., crop walk, food bank, neighborhood cleanup.
- Adopt Wake County's eight character traits and display them in your meeting place.
- Set up the expectation that your organization will be noted for character.
- Establish Community Service Awards recognizing citizenship, leadership, service, exemplary character.
- Be proactive in discussing ethics and establishing expectations for ethical behavior.
- Design "Help Your Neighbor" specific community projects that relate to character traits.
- Mentor children, e.g., big brother/big sister programs; include character traits in discussions.
- Provide positive role models, especially male role models, in the community and in the schools.
- Highlight this community as a community that values good character.
- Provide "discussion cells" to cross diverse lines within our community.
- Encourage and affirm the display of good character in youth with whom you are working.
- Adopt a school and provide mentors and tutors.
- Make sure that our entire community is aware of the character traits and understands the importance of this program.
- Provide resources to develop and implement training for teachers and parents.

Action Ideas for the Schools

- Realize that modeling good character is the best way to teach it.
- Utilize real world experience and make connections between character and success in the workplace; have businesses and community leaders come into the schools and talk to students about what characteristics they want and need in employees.
- Develop a "culture of character" in the school, so that it is evident in all aspects of the environment.
- Recognize many students - not always the same people who excel academically or athletically - affirming both progress and success.
- Develop a resource list of plays, activities, and speakers that focus on specific character traits.
- Have school groups promote character education traits, e.g., student council, National Honor Society, athletics, band.
- Provide well-designed service opportunities for children, e.g., crop walk, food bank, neighborhood cleanup, hospitals, Habitat for Humanity.
- Provide training for teachers to increase their knowledge and comfort.
- Have high expectations; be consistent across the school and school system.
- Develop innovative, experiential, character-building programs.
- Devote time on a regular basis to school instruction on morals and values.
- Welcome mentors from the community and utilize their time wisely.
- Strengthen/expand existing peer programs, e.g., peer mediation, conflict resolution, buddies.
- Feature students and how they are exhibiting good character.

Action Ideas for Students

- Make a conscious decision that modeling good character traits is a priority in your life and empower/inspire others through your enthusiasm and your actions.
- Participate in community service, e.g., crop walk, food bank, neighborhood cleanup, hospitals, Habitat for Humanity.
- Have school groups promote character education traits, e.g., student council, National Honor Society, athletics, band.
- Develop a student speakers bureau for character education presentations to younger students and civic and community organizations.
- Participate in existing community programs that develop character and leadership skills, e.g., YMCA, YWCA, Boys-Girls State, 4-H, Scouts.

Action Ideas for the Faith Community

- Devote time in sermons and children's programs to the relationship between morals, character, and behavior.
- Provide parent discussion groups or parenting classes.
- Make sure the faith community is aware of the character traits and understands the importance of this program.
- Pray for character development in our children and in our community.
- Display Wake County's list of character traits and integrate that common language into your programs.
- Recognize students and what they are doing related to character education.
- Widen your circle; reach out to children who may not be part of your congregation, especially those lacking positive role models.
- Set high expectations for character at any age, in any group, and affirm their practice.

Appendices:
Articles and
Editorials

Wake schools closer to stressing virtues

DEVELOPING THE LIST TOOK PERSEVERANCE

BY TODD SILBERMAN STAFF WRITER

When it comes to good character among Wake County students, chastity didn't make the cut.

Neither did obedience, purity of thought, hospitality or creativity.

Those are among a few dozen virtues trimmed from a list of worthy qualities assembled by a Wake schools committee asked to do what some might think impossible: agree on those traits that ought to be taught in school and stressed in the community.

The committee last week settled on eight: responsibility, respect, self-discipline, kindness, integrity, courage, perseverance and good judgment.

"If we can teach children those eight traits, we'll be able to get rid of a lot of the problems," said Ann Lee, chairman of the school system's Character Education Task Force.

The group has been meeting since December to guide the school system through a potential minefield of conflicting values and ethics.

Like dozens of school systems across the country, Wake wants to make sure that students know what it means to be a decent person.

By bringing such "character education" into the classroom, school leaders hope to counter vices such as violence and dishonesty.

"We treat symptoms rather than treating the real problem," said Lee, a former Wake assistant Principal and teacher. "The cause of a lot of problems is the lack of good character."

The first mission of the 30 board-appointed members has been to settle on a list of more than five, but less than 10, core qualities that define good character. They started with more than 60 honorable qualities before narrowing the list to eight.

"We are trying to identify common ground in the community so that we can develop a curriculum that will try and promote good character," said Daniel Heimbach, a committee member and associate professor at Southeastern Baptist Theological Seminary in Wake Forest.

The committee, Heimbach said steered clear of any values that might be considered peculiar to any group or religious sect.

Also, he said, the group has been careful to focus on those kinds of qualities for which all families would welcome support.

The next step for the group will be to agree on working definitions for the eight traits and then to circulate the list to parents and all the county's schools.

After the community offers feedback, a curriculum will be designed and put in place as early as the fall.

Reprinted with permission of The News & Observer of Raleigh, North Carolina, February 21, 1994

Chastity 'made the cut'

The Feb. 21 news article regarding the selection of virtues to be taught in our Wake County public schools obfuscated the results reached by the committee charged with choosing those virtues.

The first sentence incorrectly stated that "chastity didn't make the cut," thus implying that the committee did not consider chastity a virtue warranting inclusion in the Wake County school curriculum.

Actually, the committee decided that chastity (given the updated name of "abstinence") is a virtue that ought to be taught in schools as one aspect of self-discipline, one of the eight primary virtues selected by the committee.

The community should not be mislead. Chastity (or "abstinence") did "make the cut" and the Character Education Committee considers it to be an important aspect of a Wake County student's character.

Your reporter chose to focus his second paragraph on virtues that the committee considered but did not adopt. A more positive approach would have been to focus primary importance on the eight virtues the committee did adopt—responsibility, respect, self-discipline, kindness, integrity, courage, perseverance and good judgment. Obviously, the committee could not adopt a long list of virtues, because that would be impractical to teach and repetitive.

The virtues chosen are those which the committee believes will be universally accepted in the community as encouraging good character in students, and developing them into good citizens.

TAMI FITZGERALD Raleigh ~ The writer is a member of the Character Education Task Force of the Wake County Public Schools.

The News & Observer of Raleigh, North Carolina, February 26, 1994

Group hammers out definitions of character traits for curriculum

BY KIM WEAVER SPURR Raleigh Extra staff

"There's something wrong with our institutions, families and schools. Give me stronger families and schools and I don't care what the politics are."

TOM FETZER RALEIGH MAYOR

They may not be newspaper editors, but members of the Wake County Character Education Task Force take their editing task seriously.

They spent several hours Thursday coming up with definitions for a list of eight character traits to be implemented into the school system's curriculum next year.

They worried about sentence parallelism, pulled out dictionaries and amicably debated phrases.

At one point, as the task force moved on to the fifth word on the list —perseverance—chairman Ann Lee said, "Let's move on to perseverance, which you all are displaying at the moment." Several task force members chuckled at the remark.

At the group's last meeting, it chose the following traits as attributes worthy of being taught to Wake County students: courage, good judgment, integrity, kindness, perseverance, respect, responsibility and self-discipline. Through teaching the traits, the task force's goal is to "counter influences promoting school violence, disrespect for authority, selfishness, dishonesty and lack of discipline ..."

Several politicians showed up to watch the task force in action.

Mayor Tom Fetzer commended task force members for being willing to roll up their sleeves and promote good character.

"Bringing a child into the world is one of the most awesome responsibilities we have," he said.

"There's something wrong with our institutions, families and schools. Give me stronger families and schools and I don't care what the politics are."

Fetzer's comments were met with sporadic "Amens" from the audience.

County Commissioner Gary Pendleton told the task force the commissioners recently had passed a resolution supporting their efforts.

Before beginning the meeting, Lee clarified some information from a flier not produced by the task force. The flier indicated that a vote would be taken Thursday on abstinence as a core value.

Lee said abstinence was an outgrowth of the self-discipline character trait. A human sexuality task force is reviewing the sex education curriculum with an emphasis on abstinence, she said.

"I promise you that no one has made an attempt to hide abstinence," she said. "Our discussions have been lively, but this committee has worked beautifully and in harmony."

Pendleton threw in his own comments about abstinence.

"About 10 months ago, Apex High School decided to teach an open forum to everybody on abstinence," he said. "I thought it was great, so I made the motion [at a commissioners' meeting] we ought to commend them. It failed 5 to 2."

The task force wants community feedback about the traits. It will send home surveys to parents in April. Residents without children who wish to comment may pick up those surveys at the schools closest to their homes.

The task force holds monthly meetings on the second Thursday. They are open to the public.

Letter to the editor from a community member

The News and Observer, May 17, 1994

School survey's flip side

In response to the Wake County school system's current Character Education Survey: No citizen would respond negatively to the statements that the schools outlined, and that they propose to teach —kindness, courage, integrity, just to name a few. However, sacrifices to the academic curriculum have been omitted, and academia will be sacrificed. The survey is rigged for a unanimous vote of confidence. The public is allowed to write on a separate sheet of paper for comment. I'm sure negative comment or corrective criticism will be trashed.

I would urge Wake County citizens to pick up their pens and write in opposition to the proposed Character Education Program. In doing so we will persevere the academic curriculum our children will need to compete in their future.

Character Education

The News and Observer, May 1994

As chairman of the Character Education Task Force for the Wake County schools, I am responding to the May 17 People's Forum letter about the character education survey. I was delighted that the writer felt that "no citizen would respond negatively to the statements that the schools outlined." We have worked diligently to develop a program the entire community can support.

The writer is concerned, however, that criticism might not get a fair hearing since comments were recorded on a separate sheet. This was done to provide unlimited space for comments and to allow the response to each proposed character trait to be scored by computer, while written comments must be analyzed by hand. The task force has earnestly sought public input during this process and is committed to continued community involvement.

Secondly, the writer was concerned that character education might result in "sacrifices to the academic curriculum." The task force and the school system staff members are well aware of that potential danger. This program is not being designed as an additional subject requiring its own period. On the contrary, character education can easily be interwoven into the present curriculum.

For example, a history class might discuss the courage exhibited by our Founding Fathers; a language arts class, the way a character's integrity influenced others; a science class, the perseverance required in research; a coach, the importance of self-discipline in athletics.

I encourage the writer and other interested citizens to contact the task force for additional information.

ANNE ROBERTS LEE Raleigh

Character education

Last week our children brought home from school a Character Education Survey to be filled out by the parents. Presumably the Wake County school system wants to know what values we want them to teach our children. I feel that these should be taught in the home and not as a separate curriculum in schools.

To think that these values can be taught in a school environment the same way math and science are taught is ridiculous. How will a student get a passing grade in Perseverance, for example? What if he or she fails? Will they have to take the class again? Or maybe, since it might hurt their self-esteem, no one can fail. If that's the case, then the whole exercise is meaningless, taking yet more instructional time away from the teachers.

To even think of teaching these as subjects cheapens their meaning to students. Learning values is a life-long process that begins with the way parents treat their infants. Parents don't sit down with their kids and show them flash cards about integrity." Children observe and are molded by parents, grandparents, other child-care providers, friends and teachers.

I agree that not all children possess these qualities. Many adults do not either, and I can see why there is a reaction to try and "fix" this problem. However, many kids do have these traits and don't need character education.

I see only one way in which these values can be taught in a formalized manner in a school setting. We will have to label kids as being either character- or values-deficient, such as we label other special education needs now, and pull them out of the classroom for special instruction. This way we will not impede the learning of the majority.

Please don't slow my kids down because someone didn't learn Kindness at home.

The News
and Observer,
May 1994

Wake survey sparks questions about teaching of values

DEBBY SYKES STAFF WRITER

The results aren't tabulated yet, but some parents are wondering what 'character values' are and whether they should be included in the schools' curriculum.

Raleigh—A one page survey to the parents of every Wake County schoolchild last month asked for opinions on courage, integrity and kindness — hardly the stuff to raise controversy.

But in some cases, that's just what has happened.

The survey, which seemed designed to build support for plans to teach character values to students, has instead sparked new questions about the concept.

"My impression was, who in the hell do they think they are, and what in the world do they think they can teach my child?" Judy Keadle of Raleigh said after reading the survey. "Just the whole idea is beyond me. I cannot fathom the, blunderheads that think they're capable of critiquing my child, let alone teaching my child any moral character that she hasn't learned already."

The survey asks parents which of eight character values should be included in a new curriculum that the school system plans to begin this fall. A 32-member task force of community leaders has recommended courage, good judgment, integrity, kindness, perseverance, respect, responsibility and self-discipline.

Courage, for example, is denned as "having the determination to do the right thing- even when others don't; the strength to follow your conscience rather than the crowd. Attempting difficult things that are worthwhile."

Survey-respondents could mark the qualities they supported and also could write their suggestions on a separate page.

The surveys went to parents and educators, as well as to students in the fourth, seventh and 10th grades. The general public could pick up copies; too.

"We really felt that this needs to be a program that has broad community support," said Anne Lee, chairman of the task force. "We want to make sure we are in tune with the parents of Wake County, and I think parents want to know what's going on at school. Even if it's something they would support, if it's sort of sprung on them by surprise they might object to it."

People like Albert A. Genovesi of Cary said the survey is a waste of money because almost no one would disagree with the way it is worded. He said the school system is going to have its way anyway.

"They're self-made social engineers—who are they to experiment: with our children?" he asked.

Wake County, like a number of other school systems across the nation, is trying to solve problems like violence and dishonesty by teaching values in class.

The results of the Wake survey are being tabulated now, but Lee said she has heard very few people object.

She did tell of one father who disagreed with the principles themselves.

"He said, 'How dare we teach kindness and respect for other people?' This ' particular gentleman said he's teaching his children to be ruthless and take advantage of others first before they could take advantage of them."

The school system plans to begin teaching children the core values in the coming school year. But they won't hold separate character classes.

Instead, teachers will incorporate these values in regular classes, said Lee, who is a former teacher and assistant principal.

An English class discussing a novel, for example, could talk about the qualities a character demonstrates. Or a social studies class could analyze the values that various types of government uphold.

But Lee stressed that nothing is firmly settled and encouraged the public to attend the task force meetings on the second Thursday of the month at the Wake schools office. Although the meetings aren't open forums, she said people can speak to the members separately.

The schools also hope that other institutions in the community will help teach the values, such as churches, Scout groups and even business people. Academics alone isn't enough, she said.

"What employer would desire a highly skilled bookkeeper without integrity?" she said. "If we close our eyes and say that's the only thing that's important, then we're going to be very short-sighted."

Reprinted with permission of The News & Observer of Raleigh, North Carolina, May 21, 1994

A character lesson?

I was somewhat amused to read the Raleigh mother's salty outburst (news story, *"Wake survey sparks questions about teaching of values") in reference to proposed character studies in the Wake schools. She stated that the "blunderheads" who think they are capable of critiquing her daughter are trying to teach what the mother has already taught.

In teaching her daughter, did this mother teach her child how to "cuss"? If so, the child might need character-teaching more than ever!

Letter to the editor from a community member

The News and Observer, May 1994

Wake panel OKs 8 traits to guide students' lives

The characteristics, to be taught along with other subjects, are the stuff of Greek heroes.

By Todd Silberman, Staff Writer

Raleigh — This time next year, Wake County students may be a little more courageous, have more integrity and show more kindness. Every parent's dream child?

That noble ideal is what a Wake school committee is shooting for in a list of character traits it approved Thursday.

After about six months of deliberations, a 32-member panel of parents and educators has cleared the way for the school system to begin teaching values along with more conventional subjects such as reading and math.

The values are the stuff of Greek heroes: courage, good judgment, integrity, kindness, perseverance, respect, responsibility and self-discipline.

When it begins teaching the eight traits next year, Wake will join a growing number of school systems across the country that have adopted character education programs as an answer to such stubborn problems as violence and disrespectful students.

"As an administrator, I see this helping to focus the school," said Elvia Walker, principal of West Cary Middle School and a member of the character education committee.

"If we have a program that stresses things like honesty and integrity, the whole school will reflect that," Walker told her fellow committee members. "If we're all in the same ballpark, we'll see results."

Curriculum planners say much of the program's design remains to be worked out, but the lessons are likely to be integrated into the regular curriculum. For example, students might learn about values such as courage or integrity through a novel they are studying.

"Some traits are already covered in the curriculum," said Bill McNeal, associate superintendent for instructional services. "We're not totally reinventing the wheel here."

All students, kindergartners through high school seniors, will receive some exposure to the character program beginning in the fall, McNeal said.

The panel used a survey of parents, educators and students as an endorsement of its proposed values. Although the overall response was light, all eight of the character traits won the backing of at least 78 percent of those who answered the questionnaire. Less than 30 percent of the 105,000 surveys were returned.

Nonetheless, committee Chairman Anne Lee said the positive response was a clear signal in favor of teaching values in school.

"I'm excited that we have this support from the community," Lee said.

"I think character education is possible, because there are teachers and parents all over Wake County teaching these things right now," she said. "This gives us a vehicle to ensure that there is consistency throughout the system and that all of us agree to it."

Some parents responded to the survey by attacking the proposal to teach values in the schools, but Lee said the number of opponents was so small as to be statistically insignificant.

She said that some parents wrote that the schools should devote more time to instruction in academics and that parents should be offered classes in parenting skills.

In all, the panel received 490 written responses in addition to the surveys, ranging in length from one sentence to eight or 10 pages. About 64 percent of the letters were in support of teaching values, 26 percent were in opposition and about 10 percent were undecided.

Some members of the committee said parents remain concerned about how the values will be taught.

"There's a green light, but there's a certain caution to it," said Daniel Heimbach. "We need to look at the survey as a first step. The challenge to us is to ensure the trust of parents."

Leesville seventh-graders adopt shelter preschoolers

BY TODD SILBERMAN STAFF WRITER

RALEIGH—Schools everywhere teach simple lessons in giving at Christmas by asking students to bring canned goods or clothing to leave in a box by the classroom door or put beneath the school's tree.

But at Leesville Road Middle School this year, about 125 seventh-graders are getting a crash course in the meaning of Christmas that few food or clothing drives can convey. Coming face to face with those who make do with less is making all the difference.

"I was scared when I first went down there," said Ebony Bellamy, 13, about a visit she and her classmates made to the shelter last month. "I'd never been around homeless people before. They're just like us." Since before Thanksgiving, the students and their teachers at the suburban school in northwestern Wake County have been visiting a Raleigh shelter for families, where they have served food, played with preschoolers and made new friends.

And earlier this month, they transformed the shelter's spartan playroom into a wonderland of toys after raising more than $400— party from loose change that students donated at lunchtime. This week, they put up an "angel tree" in one of their classrooms from which to choose Christmas gifts for about 20 children who live at the shelter.

The students' teachers say that no amount of reading or classroom instruction about such values as kindness, respect and responsibility could reach the young teenagers as has their involvement with the home.

"It's really ballooned into something beautiful," said Mary Holland, a science teacher in a team of four instructors who helped conceive the project as a hands-on lesson combining character education with community service.

"It's amazing to see their reaction when they went to the shelter," she said. "It was very caring." Without the school's help, children at the home would have had to make do with the few broken toys that had been scraped together since it opened in June.

"We didn't have the money to do it," said Sylvia Wiggins, director of the Helping Hand Mission, which operates the home, known as New Bern House. "We thought it would take us two years to finish the playroom."

Not only had the students provided toys, Wiggins said, but they also were attentive to the children's educational needs by setting up writing and drawing centers, and providing such learning items as books and alphabets.

"It really jump-started us," Wiggins said. "You ought to see how excited the kids get when they go in there."

The project started after Holland began volunteering at the New Bern House this fall. She told fellow team member and math teacher Karen Beazlie about her experience, and the idea was launched to get the students involved.

"This was an opportunity to make it personal for the students," Beazlie said. We've done food drives and donated to schoolwide efforts. But it's been anonymous. "We haven't seen where it goes." This time, many of the students —part of several "teams" at the school— have made the trip to Southeast Raleigh several times. The first time was to bake cookies at Halloween.

"They're much more motivated," Beazlie said. "They can connect with individual children."

Still, she said, she had little insight just how interested the students would be.

"I really had no idea," Beazlie said early this month, as she stood in her classroom piled high with toys a few days before Operation Playroom" swung into action. There were a play kitchen, a rocking horse, tape players and dazes of stuffed animals.

Beazlie had even incorporated the project into her math lesson for the day, with students using a scale floor plan of the room to design the layout of toys, bookshelves and play areas.

"I just thought it would be a good idea to give them a chance to reach out to others," Beazlie said. "I think this age group is really good at that. They just need the opportunity."

The students say the project has opened a window on the world with which they'd had little or no first-hand experience.

"That area — it's different from North Raleigh," said Tara Cates, 13. "I usually don't thing of Raleigh as a place where homeless people live. It made me realize what's really out there."

Lauren Peele, 12, said the project has been a lesson in humility for her.

"It doesn't really get to you until you see it for real," Lauren said. "It makes you think about what you have and they don't."

THE PEOPLE'S FORUM
Why no students?

As a student at East Wake High School, I want to give a student's opinion on the article "Wake panel OKs 8 value traits for schools" I was appalled that the 32-member panel to discuss values did not include any students. It would have been common courtesy to include the people most directly affected.

The News and Observer, July 7, 1994

Students on task force

I read with interest the recent People's Forum letter from an East Wake High School student who is concerned about Character Education. He questioned why we had no student representation on our 32-member Wake County Character Education Task Force. I want to set the record straight: We have had three students on board since the Task Force's inception last year. Two are high school students and one is a middle school student.

Students have been part of the process since the beginning. They helped guide the selection of character traits. When we surveyed the community, we included all of Wake County's fourth, seventh and tenth graders. As we move into the implementation phase, students will play a large role in guiding the focus of Character Education is every school.

I am delighted that students are giving so much thought to Character Education. There is no question that support from the community—parents, business people, civic groups, churches, schools and students—is critical to Character Education's success.

The new school year will be an exciting time, and I hope everyone in Wake County understands that each of us has a responsibility to our young people.

ANNE LEE Chairman Character Education Task Force Raleigh

The News and Observer, July 9, 1994

Values education pays off

Does values education have positive effects? Indeed it does, according to the evaluation of Jefferson Center's pilot program in the Los Angeles schools. Here are some of the key findings of surveys conducted before and after the values education program was in place:

• Discipline problems declined sharply, especially tardiness (down 40 percent), minor discipline problems (down 39 percent), and major disciplinary problems such as fighting, drugs, or weapons (down 25 percent).

• According to principals, student responsibility rose. Students tended to act more responsibly, did not blame others, resisted peer pressure, and generally understood the concepts of respect and honesty.

• Teachers reported that the program provokes good classroom discussions, provides a systematic approach to teaching values and responsibility, and helps students become aware of their choices, take responsibility for their actions, and enhance their self-esteem.

In addition, the behavioral changes among students affected the learning climate at participating schools.

• Student participation in extracurricular activities rose, as did the number of students on the honor roll.

• Teachers gave high ratings to the curriculum's ease of implementation and to the common language and value system it provides, which they said enhances teacher-student communication. When asked what they gained from the experiment, the teachers listed a greater sense of satisfaction and accomplishment, stronger motivation and greater self-esteem, a clarification of their own thinking, and a foundation for better communication with their students.

• Administrators' attitudes toward values education also took a positive shift. At the beginning of the project, 90 percent expressed a strong belief in the benefits of values education, and 80 percent thought teachers should devote more time to it. At the end of the yearlong pilot, 100 percent of the respondents expressed a strong belief in the benefits of values education, and 92 percent said teachers should spend more time on it. The data indicate the principals' support for values education grew even stronger after they experimented with it on a schoolwide basis.

B.D.B. and M.E.K.

The American School Board Journal, December. ©1992, The National School Boards Association. All rights reserved.

CHARACTER DEVELOPMENT GROUP offers complete resources including publications and staff development training for the planning, implementation and assessment of an effective character education program in school systems.

Other titles for character education practitioners...

Order Form

Book Title

Book Title	Quantity	Price	Total
CHARACTER EDUCATION WORKBOOK A "How-To" Manual for School Boards, Administrators & Community Leaders		$12.00	
TEACHING CHARACTER Idea Books for Middle-School Grades		$24.00	
Teacher's Idea Book		$24.00	
Parent's Idea Book		$12.00	
RULES AND PROCEDURES The First Step in School Civility		$14.00	
PROMISING PRACTICES IN CHARACTER EDUCATION Nine Success Stories from Across The Country		$12.00	
DEVELOPING CHARACTER IN STUDENTS A Primer for Teachers, Parents & Communities		$12.95	
LESSONS FROM THE ROCKING CHAIR Timeless Stories For Teaching Character		$12.00	

Subtotal	
NC Tax (6%)	
Shipping Total	
Total	

SHIPPING:
Up to $25 ....$4
$25 to $100 ....$6
Over $100 .... 6%

Form of payment: ☐ **Check** ☐ **PO** #_____

Make checks payable to:
Character Development Group, PO Box 9211, Chapel Hill, NC 27515-9211

Ship To:

Name _____

Organization _____ Title _____

Address _____

City: _____ State: _____ Zip: _____

Phone: (__) _____ Signature: _____

FAX ORDERS: (919) 967-2139

For further information, or to schedule a Character Development Workshop, call **(919) 967-2110**, or e-mail to **Respect96@aol.com.**
(Call regarding quantity discounts)